ALTERITY

The Experience of The Other

Clive Hazell
©2009

AuthorHouse™
1663 Liberty Drive
Bloomington, IN 47403
www.authorhouse.com
Phone: 1-800-839-8640

© 2009 Clive Hazell. All rights reserved.

No part of this book may be reproduced, stored in a retrieval system, or transmitted by any means without the written permission of the author.

First published by AuthorHouse 7/23/2009

ISBN: 978-1-4389-7183-4 (e)
ISBN: 978-1-4389-7182-7 (sc)

Library of Congress Control Number: 2009906484

Printed in the United States of America
Bloomington, Indiana

This book is printed on acid-free paper.

Dedication

I dedicate this book to my father, for his many edifying discourses.

Acknowledgements

I thank my wife, Rosalinda, for her patience as I pondered these issues. I also thank my friends at the Kazimierz Dabrowski Symposium, for their warmth, openness and support. As usual, many thanks are due to Shawna Foose for her editing and Marilyn Hallett at Michigan Office Services for typing.

Contents

Introduction

    A: Alterity as a Psychological Construct   xiii

    B: Definition of Alterity   xvii

I. Approaches to Alterity

    A: Psychology and Alterity   3

    B: Philosophy and Alterity   19

    C: Religion and Alterity   35

    D: Social Science and Alterity   38

    E: Art and Alterity   47

    F: The Physiology of Alterity   53

II. Alterity: Clinical Applications

    A: Alterity and Psychotherapy   58

    B: Clincal Examples: Individuals   62

    C: Clinical Examples: Alterity and Groups   71

    D. Trauma, Groups and Alterity   83

III. Alterity All Around

    A: A Potpourri of Experiences of Alterity   88

    B: The Social Management of Alterity   95

	C: Sex and Alterity	100
IV.	Lacan and Alterity	
	A: Circuits of Alterity	107
	B: The Phallic Organizer	113
	C. Theorists Influenced by Lacan	122
V.	TPD: An Integrative Framework	
	A. The Theory of Positive Disintegration	132
	A. Correspondences of Forms of Alterity with Levels of TPD	138
II.	Where is the Object?	
Appendix: Alterity and Emptiness	147
References And Bibliography	149

Introduction

"Then something even more extraordinary happened. My perception shifted, and for a moment I was the immensity of the stars perceiving the infinite in my physical body. I could see myself in the middle of the desert—so small. I saw that my physical body was made of billions of tiny stars, which I knew were atoms, and they were as vast as all of the stars in the sky.

That night, I knew that the infinite inside my physical body is just a continuation of the infinite all around me. I am part of the infinite all around me. I am part of that infinite, and so is every object I perceive. There is no difference between any of us, or between us and any object."

(Don Miguel Ruiz, 2004, 46-7)

"The simple but empirically determined consciousness of my own existence proves the existence of objects in space outside myself."

(Kant, 1781, 1787)

A: Alterity as a Psychological Construct

"The ego needs the Thou in order to become a Self."
Otto Rank, 1941, p. 290

The word "alterity" rarely shows up in psychology books. The Penguin (2002) and the Oxford (2009) dictionaries of psychology do not refer to it. Large numbers of psychologists do not seem to know the meaning of the word (thus the extended title of this book). Also uncommon is usage of the term "otherness." Yet the whole of psychology is suffused with concepts that are intimately related to, or even based upon, assumptions about alterity. In turn, these concepts form parts of theories. These theories affect beliefs, and these, in their turn affect action in all the domains of psychology. Thus, many (if not all) psychological theories are operating on a conceptual basis that is unexamined or not made explicit. Much of the time, it appears that psychological theories operate as if the concept of alterity is stable and settled. It is taken for granted that a certain set of assumptions about self and other are such "common sense" that there is no need to uncover this assumptive base, make it explicit and thus locate the theory in relation to the various notions regarding self and other.

Thus, it is the purpose of this book to describe various sets of assumptions regarding the phenomenon of alterity, to demonstrate the impact these differing assumptions have on theory (and thus action) and to propose a general theory of alterity that will aid in the organization of this concept. This theory will be yoked to Lacanian ideas and

Dabrowski's theory of positive disintegration. This final position will assert that different notions of alterity occur in different registers and on a developmental continuum. By extension, psychological theories based on different conceptions of alterity will be applicable to specific regions of this developmental continuum and different Lacanian registers.

The overall approach of this book is similar to that taken in *The Experience of Emptiness* (Hazell, 2003), where a largely philosophical or religious idea is examined and defined and an attempt is made to connect it to the corpus of psychological thought. Thus, in Chapter one, the concept of alterity is examined from a series of perspectives: psychological, philosophical, artistic and religious. In Chapter two, clinical applications for counseling individuals and groups are examined. The aim here is to demonstrate the practical utility and application of the ideas explored in Chapter one. In Chapter three, "Alterity All Around," a somewhat freewheeling approach is taken up as inspired by Benjamin's "Arcade Project" (2002). Alterity is examined in a variety of contexts. Finally, in chapters four and five, an attempt is made to organize the widely disparate notions of alterity with Lacanian theory and Dabrowski's theory of positive disintegration.

The concept of alterity is a key concept in the study of behavior, yet its meaning and usage has been taken for granted. It underlies multiple theories and related concepts routinely deployed in psychology, for example; autonomy, separation individuation, locus of control, enmeshment, differentiation, attribution, prejudice, scapegoating, projective identification and individuation, to name a few. To embark on theoretical ventures without first clarifying the underlying nature of such a basic concept seems ill-advised. This volume aims to examine this concept and suggest an organizing template for the idea of alterity.

I hope to show that there are multiple alterities, that the various theories of psychology utilize one or several of these concepts of alterity, and that these multiple alterities are usefully organized by Dabrowski's theory of positive disintegration, combined with extremely useful clarifications from Lacan and Levinas.

Definition of Alterity

The concept of alterity has a number of different shadings of meaning. I would like, here, to "shave off" some additional meanings that have become attached to the concept of alterity so that, for the purposes of this study, we have a delimited, fairly focused definition.

Here, the term "alterity" simply means the state or quality of being other, or of not being of the self. As such, the term implies the recognition and discrimination of the categories of self and other. While it is assumed that the very nature of this discrimination alters with time, place and person such that self and other might be seen as fused, separate, radically separate, transcendentally connected or not discriminated at all, additional evaluations of self and other are not included in this definition. What is under examination here is alterity pure and simple. It may be (and some have argued) that this is a specious and impossible separation, for the very recognition of alterity necessitates such phenomena as devaluation, negation or marginalization of the other. The position held here, however, is that while these evaluations frequently (perhaps usually) are accompaniments of the recognition of alterity, they need not necessarily be, and to include them in a study of alterity too early in the process of thinking it through causes unnecessary confusion.

The following seven points further elaborate and clarify the definition of the concept of alterity as it will be used here.

a) Although the antonym of "other" is often "same" as in "self same," and although difference often alerts us to alterity, alterity and difference are not coterminous in meaning. One could be aware of an "identical other" or an imaginary twin.

b) Although the other is frequently disparaged or despised and seen as inferior to self, this is not always the case. Often enough, the other is idealized or worshipped. Equally, the other could be viewed as neutral or "OK." The other does not always have to be scapegoated and used as a repository for unwanted elements of the self nor, even if the other is so used, does it have to be so used unconsciously or with degradation.

c) Further, even though the other is often silent or silenced, this does not always have to be the case. It is possible to have a very vocal other, the other that will not be quiet.

d) While several writers have equated, or more accurately, conflated alterity with marginality, this conflation does not always have to be the case. One could have a "central other" as in the others that are in the "in crowd" when one finds oneself on the margins. Furthermore, alterity can exist in a neutral space, almost bland in its value-free discrimination of self and object.

e) Alterity is part of reality, as well as part of the real, referring here to Lacan's tripartite notation of "registers" of Real, Symbolic and Imaginary (1977, 1981, 1993). The alterity of the Real is beyond us, only apprehended in moments of "tuché" when in an uncanny fashion a real event seems to coincide with the social constructions of reality. The Real is the "thing in itself" (of Kantian philosophy); absent symbols, absent imagination, it is complete, gapless and unapprehendable. The *concept* of alterity does not belong in this set.

f) The concept of alterity is just that, a concept. It thus belongs largely in the domain of the symbolic, the domain of language. The symbolic overlaps with and interacts with the Imaginary of Lacan. Concepts and ideas are infused, to a greater or lesser extent, with imaginary components, often powered by emotion. In addition, concepts themselves often are derived from imaginary phenomena. Thus the concept of alterity can be found as a "pure" concept, almost algebraic in its logical purity, and it can also be found in forms that are saturated with imaginary components, laden with fantasies and emotion, fantasies of persecution, humiliation, dread, victory and love. Alterity as a concept in the symbolic register also overlaps with alterity in the Real. For example, an extreme phenomenon of nature, such as a storm or a magnificent landscape, can suddenly make us aware of radical "otherness."

We have, I hope, accomplished the task of "shaving off" the additional meanings often adhering to the concept of alterity and reduced it, for the current examination, to the bare bones of its meaning, the state or quality of being other. This apprehension of alterity may quickly become suffused with meanings and may take multiple forms. The understanding of these is of vital importance in the comprehension of human relationships. These additional meanings, however, are regarded here as superstructure built upon, in complex ways, the substructure of the basic concept of alterity. We see, further, how the meaning of alterity shifts as we migrate through the Lacanian domains of the Real, the Imaginary and the Symbolic. The examination of these additional meanings will form much of the substance of this book. We begin with an examination of the treatment of the concept of alterity from a variety of perspectives. To yoke these abstract ideas to the everyday, following is a vignette aimed at capturing aspects of the experience of alterity. This vignette anticipates several of the themes to be explored later.

Getting Splashed

I am running on a sidewalk alongside one of my favorite parks in Chicago, feeling good. The air is fresh and aromatic with wet soil after a recent rain. A car, coming up from behind, swerves close by, right through a long, deep puddle. A translucent grey curtain of water arcs in slow motion over my head and slaps down on me, cold and smelly. The deluge seems to go on forever. Finally, it stops and the car, an old blue beater, swerves back out into the middle of the road, steaming from its excursion through the puddle.

I decide to act as though nothing had happened and thus deprive the prankster of any further fun, even though I am soaked to the skin. Violent fantasies surge through my mind and body. The car disappears down Irving Park Road. Gradually my pure anger subsides and it is replaced with angry psychoanalysis. It was a young man, I argue, symbolically attacking/urinating on/ejaculating on his father/mother as he drove his sad blue phallus down the street. He both longs for and hates his father. I fantasize as to how I could make him anxious by inflicting these "interpretations" of his conflicted homoeroticism upon him.

And then these ideas vaporize as I realize that this was an experience of radical alterity. As I was running, I was like a happy child at play, continuous and at one with my world. Suddenly, a sharp inundation wakes me up, makes me radically aware of the Other. This awareness is accompanied by a flood of emotions and defenses against them. Further, while this was my experience, the whole event can be understood as a piece of performance art, put on, probably unconsciously, by the young driver to let me, and the world, know of his history in regard to the experience of alterity. And what he is saying is this: *"It was too much, too soon; it hit me unawares. It filled me with helpless rage. I was left unutterably alone. That is how it was and still is with me and the Other."*

Chapter I: Approaches to Alterity

"Oneself as Another" suggests from the outset that the selfhood of oneself implies otherness to such an intimate degree that one cannot be thought of without the other, that instead one passes into the other, as we might say in Hegelian terms.

Ricoeur (1992, p.3)

"Glory be to God for dappled things-
For skies of couple-colour as a brinded cow;
For rose-moles all in stipple upon trout that swim;
Fresh-firecoal chestnut falls; finches' wings;

Gerard Manley Hopkins "Pied Beauty" (1876 – 1889)

"Hell is other people"

Sartre , "Huis Clos" (1987)

Clive Hazell

This chapter reviews the idea of alterity as it has been treated in a variety of disciplines; psychology, philosophy, religion, social psychology, anthropology, art and physiology. Clearly, in such a slim volume these studies are not exhaustive. The reader, however, will become acquainted with the breadth of meanings and applications of the concept. Perhaps this will induce a deeper sense of the complexity of the phenomenon and even a certain wish for organization. Such organization is satisfactorily provided by Dabrowski's theory, as explicated in chapter five in combination with ideas from Lacan and Levinas.

A: Psychology and Alterity

"Psyche! From thee they spring O life of Time and all Alterity!"

H. More, "Song of Soul" (1642)

There appear to be, broadly speaking, seven approaches to the concept of alterity in the field of psychology. These approaches, while each having their distinct characteristics, can often overlap or work in concert. This section, without examining the fine detail of the theories involved, describes the outlines of the theory of alterity contained in each of these seven theories, or "theory groups." My conclusion is that each of these approaches is reasonably valid for the given realm, for the given form of alterity. The titles for each of these approaches have been selected in an attempt to capture their essence.

1. Normal Autism – Symbiosis - Separation

The theory that there is a developmental progression from "self with no other" (normal autism, primary narcissism or the preobjectal state) to "self and other" fused together in a symbiosis to a state of "self separate from other" is expounded in the theory of Margaret Mahler (1975). Tustin (1972, 1990) focuses attention on the very early states of this sequence while Searles (1979) focuses on the symbiotic phase and its clinical consequences in the treatment of schizophrenia. Masterson (1972) addresses the vicissitudes of the "rapprochement phase" in separation sequence and its role in the etiology and treatment of "borderline personality disorder."

Mahler's theory offers a rich and intricate, empirically based model of the development of the sense of the other. She documents, for example, very interesting physiological correlates of the separation-individuation process. The trunk of the body, over which the baby begins to get some control at about the age of six months, helps the baby to physically and psychologically separate from the symbiotic bonding with the mother, to literally draw back and take her in as a separate person. In addition, this shift of differentiation is accompanied by a more focused, alert look in the infant's eyes—the "hatched look."

Shortly after this, Mahler documents Spitz's (1965) notion of "stranger anxiety" and this can be understood as the baby's encounter with someone who is not mother, someone who is disturbingly other. Often, in response to the mother's absence, Mahler observed the child enter a "low keyed state" where the child becomes muted in her emotions and avoids eye contact with the other as if even witnessing the other would be to acknowledge their separateness from their mother.

The "other" thus emerges through a developmental sequence. This sequence ends for these theories in clearly established self-other boundaries, with perhaps a few regressions to autistic-like or symbiotic states. This theory of the development of the concept of self and other serves as an influential "road map" for much clinical theory which is based on supporting the differentiated self-other boundary and the functionality seen to accompany it. Masterson (1972) provides an excellent example of this approach.

2. **Permeable self-permeable other**

In contrast with the relatively well-sealed-off self and other of the previous group of theories, we find a group of thinkers who posit an

Alterity: The Experience of the Other

ongoing permeability existing at an unconscious level between self and other as a universal human process. They even go so far as to argue that to lack such permeability is to lack a deep connection with others via projective identification and introjection. This results in one being "out of touch" and is risky not only for one's own mental health, but also for the mental health of others, especially if those others are children, students, patients or clients.

Thus, Melanie Klein (1935,1946,2002) and thinkers influenced by her such as Bion (1959,1961,1977, 1997) and Rosenfeld (1965) seem to pose not the rigorously well-bounded self and other, but a self and other seemingly separate at the conscious level but still, throughout all life, fused with the other and vigorously, often confusedly and passionately, exchanging elements of self and other.

This concept of self and other is also present in the object relations theory of W.R.D. Fairbairn (1952) and more recently in the work of Robert Langs (1978) especially in his conception of the Type B communicative field.

Several ideas of Bion's, although they do not explicitly mention the concept of alterity relate strongly to the topic and are worthy of examination here. Perhaps first amongst these would be his concept of "O," which can perhaps be regarded as a non concept that lies behind all concepts. This idea seems to imply that there is that which is beyond explanation. (This is perhaps hardest for psychologists to admit: that there are behaviors, people, and relationships that lie beyond the explanatory scope of existing theories.)

Since these phenomena are external to our powers of explanation, they are experienced as <u>other</u>. This is difficult to accept – not only because of the humility of saying, "I do not know," but also because saying you do not know is to accept radical alterity. Thus the quest to increase knowledge (K) can be seen not only as a quest for mastery, but also as a quest to diminish or eradicate the experience of radical alterity which humans can experience as a slap in the face or as a chilling reminder of finitude. There are, of course, alternative reactions to this alterity (finitude). Omniscience or, on a lesser scale, being a "know it all" is one way of blocking the experience of alterity arising from the finitude of one's knowledge. Another technique would be to (solipsistically) deny the very existence of knowledge. Following this logic, if there is no knowledge then there can be no ignorance, thus the experience of alterity is again pre-empted. Related to this technique would be the identification with a superior being who is omniscient. Thus, by proxy, one evades the experience of alterity.

A "middle ground" position might be found in the individual who obsessively quests for absolute mastery in their field. They recognize the otherness of that which is not known but set out to claim it for themselves, so that it no longer is other. Bit by bit the otherness of that which is not known is claimed for the self. Of course as each bit is claimed, further horizons of the unknown emerge and the would-be knower may come to recognize the infinity or the unboundedness of their task. In the face of this realization some may continue in the never-ending Sisyphean task for mastery. Some may recoil into the previously mentioned defensive maneuvers. Thus, learning style and learning motivation might be affected by one's underlying sense of and attitude towards the various forms of the experience of alterity.

Kohut's notion of the "selfobject," in addition to his assumption that such self-object fusion is lifelong, fits into this category of alterity theory. His findings about the transactions within the selfobject unit are different from Klein, perhaps largely because he is exploring different dynamics.

Alterity, the sense of self and other, is dealt with in two ways by Freud, and most other dynamic psychologists. Alterity in the realm of secondary process thinking (the focal, rational, linear, aim-inhibited thinking that accepts the reality principle) is the conventional division of self and other. Self is self; other is other. There is communication between self and other. Perhaps this communication is conscious, perhaps unconscious, but self and other, apart from this, are separate.

In the unconscious, however, or in the realm of primary process thinking (wish fulfilling thinking not curbed by the reality principle) self and other are not so separated. Self and other in primary process thinking can fuse into one; can change places so that self becomes other and other, self. Self and other can be distributed across many selves, many objects. Self or other can also be "disguised" by being made into a third person or object. The self and other of primary process is the self and other of dreams, of compressions, reversals, wish fulfillments, displacements and dispersals described in *The Interpretation of Dreams* (1900).

Freud's paper, "The Uncanny" (2003) also touches upon the theme of alterity, yet from a perspective that turns out to have great therapeutic importance. One interpretation of the uncanny is that it is an experience that contains elements that symbolize the repressed. The repressed can be understood as that which is wished to be alteric, that which is wished not to belong, to be, in the literal sense, *unheimlich* ("unhomely"). However, sometimes the repressed revisits us in our waking life; it taps on the door of consciousness and this experience of the revisitation of the repressed is felt to be paradoxically as radically alteric and familiar, as uncanny. Since that which is repressed is traumatic in some form or other, we have here a neat linkage with several other ideas to be explored later; insofar as Taussig (1992) and Hopper (2003), posit a link between the experience of alterity and trauma. Taussig argues that all unanticipated misfortune is experienced as alteric.

Thus, with Freud, the experience of self and other rides upon the type of thinking one is engaging in, primary process or secondary process. Interestingly, one might posit that some individuals will have greater or lesser access to these two types of thinking and thus will have greater or lesser access to the two differing sets of conceptualizations of self and other. It is argued, later in this book, that an increased capacity to oscillate, at will, as it were from one "phase" to another, from primary to secondary and back again, is not only, as has been widely argued, a sign of a well-analyzed or creative person, but is also a sign of emotional development as depicted in the theory of positive disintegration (Dabrowski *et al*, 1970, 1977).

3. Self and Other as Interpersonal Construction

Potentially overlapping with these approaches is the set of theories that posit that the concepts of "self" and "other" are the result of an interpersonal process itself. H.S. Sullivan's interpersonal theory sits squarely in this tradition while the social constructionist approach of Berger and Luckman (1991) provides a social psychological perspective. The intersubjective theory of Mitchell (1988) also falls into this category; "self" and "other" are constructions occupying an intermediary social space.

Hartmann (1991) provides a rare empirical set of studies that address or come close to addressing the topic of alterity. The word "alterity" does not occur in the text since the major concern is with personal boundaries, both inner and outer. Hartmann has developed a seemingly robust measure of boundaries that is comprised, in its proposed form, of several factors. One of the proposed factors is "interpersonal" and has to do with what is here being termed alterity, including such items as, "I feel at one with the world," and, "I feel very separate and distinct from everyone else." The scale as a whole (which measures both internal and external boundaries) holds together significantly and bears many plausible relationships with several other variables of great interest. While several significant subscales do emerge from the factor analytic study of the measure, none of these factors can be argued to measure the dimension of alterity as here defined. The interpersonal dimension does not seem to survive as such and the items seem to be scattered over several other factors—factors that include boundaries between sleep and waking; between thoughts, feelings and moods; between childhood, adolescence and adulthood and so on. The general boundary factor ("Sumbound") is thus comprised of a wide concatenation of boundaries inside and outside the person. This Sumbound factor does manifest many interesting correlations with other variables of psychological significance, and since several "alterity" items are contained in this factor it is of interest to note some of these.

Hartmann finds that thin boundaries might be more prevalent in those diagnosed with schizophrenia or schizotypal personality disorder, while thicker boundaries might be found in persons diagnosed with obsessive-compulsive features. He also suggests that thin boundaries might increase hypnotic suggestibility. He finds that, in his population, women tended to have thinner boundaries and that thinner boundaries might be found in persons who are more "sensitive" to stimuli. In very intriguing sections, he conjectures that thin boundaries might be associated with lower levels of norepinephrine in the frontal cortex; thicker boundaries being associated with alertness, focused thinking and higher levels of norepinephrine. Not fully explored by Hartmann, but certainly posited as a possibility is the potential for trauma to affect thickness of boundaries. I would hypothesize, following Hopper (2003), that boundaries can either become very thick or very thin in response to trauma, and that trauma has the tendency to "lock" the person into a certain range of thinness or thickness. It becomes difficult for the person who has been traumatized to alter their boundaries depending on their situation and the task at hand. This results in a corresponding loss of adaptability. Hartmann also hypothesizes that certain psychotropic drugs influence boundaries. For example, uppers—cocaine, crack, "crystal meth" create thicker boundaries while LSD creates thinner boundaries.

Hartmann's study is extremely provocative, especially since it has so many linkages with other theories. In addition to those hinted at above, I would like also to propose Dabrowski's theory (1970). Hartmann's notions regarding "sensitivity" seem extremely close to Dabrowski's concept of overexcitability. By substitution we can argue that higher levels of overexcitability will lead to thinner boundaries (other things being equal, for example, exposure to trauma) and that lower levels of overexcitabilities will lead to thicker boundaries. The type of boundary thinness will be predicated upon the overexcitability profile. For example, individuals with high psychomotor overexcitabilities will have thinner boundaries when it comes to bodily movement and gesture. People with higher emotional overexcitabilities will have thinner boundaries with regard to the feelings of themselves and others. According to Dabrowski's theory, emotional overexcitability is what propels development to higher levels, oftentimes potentiating positive disintegration. Thus we would predict, according to this line of reasoning, that incidences of thinner emotional boundaries will be significantly higher in those at higher levels of emotional development in Dabrowski's scheme.

Belonging also in this constructivist explication of alterity is the theory of Piaget (1969, 1976) which places the formation of the schema of the object and object permanence as the key accomplishment of the sensory motor stage of development. Thus, Piaget asserts that;

> *"In the course of the first eighteen months, however, there occurs a kind of Copernican revolution, or, more simply, a kind of radical decentering process whereby the child eventually comes to regard himself as an object among others in a universe that is made up of permanent objects (that is, structured in a spatio-temporal manner) and in which there is at work a causality that is both localized in space and objectified in things.*
>
> *(Piaget and Inhelder, 1969, p13)*

Prior to this acquisition of the concept of the permanent object, the child acts, upon the object's disappearance, "as if the object had been reabsorbed." (Piaget and Inhelder, 1969, p. 14). Thus for Piaget, the origin of the concept of alterity lies in the developmental processes occurring in the first eighteen months of life. These developmental processes involve the dynamics of assimilation and accommodation, which in turn depend upon the child having an active interaction with his or her environment.

Piaget's use of the metaphor, "Copernican revolution" reminds us that such a development will be accompanied by an array of emotional responses that will affect the outcome of this radical shift. Freud remarks that the Copernican revolution is the "first insult" to humanity's narcissism (the following insults being delivered by Darwin and Freud himself) while Laplanche (1999) discusses the concept of alterity in an article with the subtitle, "The Copernican Revolution Unfinished."

4. **Self and Other as Extensions of Collective Unconscious**

In this framework self and other gain in their apparent separation as development unfolds but are only separate at the level of the conscious and personal unconscious. All selves and others are fused at the level of the collective unconscious. This position is most clearly expounded upon by C.G. Jung (1971, 1993). It is also intimated in the work of Maslow when he describes, for example, the "oceanic feeling" (the feeling of oneness with the universe) as being quite common among self-actualizing people.

While many other psychodynamic theories posit that self and other may communicate with one another unconsciously, and thus be connected via communication, this set of theories posits that self and other are, in addition, connected by a structure such as the collective unconscious of Jung. At times, this structure is argued to exist at a higher dimension of time and space. Thus, following the argument (found in "Flatland" (Abbott, 2008) and in Ouspensky, of "Tertium Organum" (1998)) that objects that appear to be separate in lower dimensions frequently turn out to be connected when viewed from

Alterity: The Experience of the Other

higher dimensions, self and other (seeming separate in four dimensional space time) are connected in higher dimensions of space and time.

The clinical and theoretical consequences of this way of thinking about alterity are considerable. For example, the experience of a sense of oneness with others or of a sense of knowing someone else's thoughts and feelings without words could be seen not only as a regression to symbiotic modes of relating but also as a making of contact with others through the collective unconscious.

This approach to self and other is analogous to Bion's understanding of groups (1961). Bion posits a group mentality, which seems to operate in a manner approximately similar to a collective unconscious for a small group operating under certain conditions. This group mentality can operate according to certain valences for basic assumptions (dependency, fight-flight or pairing) and these basic assumption groups affect behavior in the group. Thus the individual in the group is operating under a form of alterity that is different from the conventional understanding. Although the individual may feel isolated and separated from others, he is connected to these others through the medium of the group mentality and is perhaps expressing the will of the group mentality in behaviors that he takes to be of his own authorship, but which are, in large part or small, the result of forces operating in this group unconscious. In these approaches then, the separation of self and other is analogous to the separation of, say, the continents. While on one level they are separate, on a deeper level they are connected and interactive.

5. **Phenomenological Self, Phenomenological Other**

There is a body of thought in psychology that, following a phenomenological-pragmatic approach, addresses the issue of self and other from an experiential viewpoint. The self is that which, in the phenomenal field, is experienced as the "proprium," that which belongs to oneself. No rules are laid down in this approach as to which elements should or should not be in the proprium and the boundaries of self and other could be quite fluid. Similarly, no *a priori* concepts are provided for elements in self and other or as to its dynamics since this approach, in its purest form, is thoroughly phenomenological. Examples of this theory would be Carl Rogers' personality theory (1961) and Gordon Allports' work (1955).

Rogers does not explicitly tackle the concept of alterity in his writings but one can discern trends in his thinking. A secure sense of separation of self and object is seen to be essential for empathic understanding to occur. "When I can freely feel this strength of being a separate person, then I find I can let myself go much more deeply in understanding him because I am not fearful of losing myself." (Rogers, 1961, p. 52)

Empathy is not seen as creating a unity of self and other for two reasons; a) it can often be "bumbling and faulty" (1961, p.53) and b) one approaches the other with an acceptance not only of what they are in the here and now (which is a complex process, in many ways unreachable) but also in their potential, which is unknown. Rogers quotes Buber. "Confirming means…accepting the whole potentiality of the other…" This potentiality is an unknown quantity. Rogers outlines the trends he sees as these potentials unfold, but the potentials of the self are emergent; they are "by their very nature unpredictable in their specifics." (1961).

It is in this last that Rogers seems to join Levinas (1969, 1987, 2000, 2006) in his conception of alterity insofar as there always left in the other a residuum of mystery. Empathy can only go so far in "capturing" the other. For Levinas this mystery, however, is transcendent.

6. Positivist Self, Positivist Other

Psychology generated in the positivist-empirical tradition is largely unipsychic (as opposed to polypsychic, not involving multiple personalities) in its approach. Self and other are viewed as unitary phenomena. In addition, since sense data (upon which positivist-empirical theories are built) point so convincingly towards separate selves, self and other are regarded as being, in fact, separate. Self and other might be connected by exchanges of symbols and other measurable phenomena but invisible or immeasurable connections do not form part of theories developed in this tradition.

Examples of such theories would be most of those in the Behaviorist and Cognitive-Behaviorist tradition: Skinner (1976), Watson (2008), Beck (1979) Bandura and Walters (1963). Even Dollard and Miller's (1950) admirable attempt to integrate behavioristic and psychodynamic theory belongs in this constellation.

Interestingly, this paradigm is quite congruent with legalistic constructions of self and other. Many legal puzzles can be framed as conflicts over which paradigm of self and other should be adopted. Ones involving "multiple personality" (assumptions of polypsychism) or of diminished responsibility resulting from undue influence from others would be examples of such conundrums.

7. Self and Other in the Field of Language

The prime example of this approach to the problem of self and other is in the work of Lacan (1977, 1981, 1993). In this frame, self and other are found in the interacting fields of the "Real," "Imaginary" and the "Symbolic"—in the field of language which pre-exists the self and the other. We are, from the origin, caught inextricably in a web of language out of which is created an imaginary-symbolic self and other. This creates a felt "reality" of self and other. This reality is to be discriminated from the "Real" of self and other, for the domain of the "Real" is unapprehendable directly. It is only "seen" via representations in the registers of the "Imaginary" and "Symbolic" which then constitute reality.

To differentiate this approach from one that may seem the same, namely, the "Interpersonal" or "Constructivist" approach to self and other, we note that there are very significant divergences in that language is viewed as a pre-existing matrix which, with its rules, places *a priori* limitations on the processes of self-other construction. Language has, as it were, a powerful, overarching, inescapable autonomy. It is not seen as a tool or device which the subject controls. We are the subjects of language and it determines us.

In addition, this approach is different insofar as it radically "decenters" the subject. In the Lacanian view, the notion of the unitary self is not accepted. So far this is in accord with most psychodynamic views which accept the notion of multiple selves (polypsychism) of varying degrees of intrapsychic connectedness. Along with this idea, of course, goes the notion of "multiple others" and, thus multiple selves (some conscious, some unconscious) in relation to multiple others (some conscious, some unconscious). Lacan, however, goes beyond this insofar as these multiplicities are "seen" not so much as located within the individual (in their depths, as it were) but distributed across the communicational field. Self and other are multiple and distributed. This realization is distressing and is thus relegated to the unconscious. Other beliefs about self and other are therefore regarded as defensive, as *falsifying functions of the ego*. One of the major functions of Lacanian psychoanalysis, therefore, is to interrupt this falsifying function and to engender true speech, that is, to bring about a situation where the individual talks about him or herself and others in a manner that recognizes self and other as immersed in the field of language. Lacan offers symbols to capture and signify these two forms of the other: *l'Autre, grand A,* and *l'autre petit a* (meaning the Other with a big "O" and the other with a little "o").

The Other with a big O is the Other (the sense of alterity) found in the symbolic register. This Other is the Other of laws, of the laws of language, the rules of symbol systems and communication. This Other is the Other of the prohibition of lawlessness. It is a castrating Other, the Other of the "paternal function." This Other is radically Other, very separate from the self. It is the Other of the state.

The other with a little o (*l'autre petit a*) is the other of the imaginary register. This other is conceptually close to the symbiotic other of Mahler (1975) or the selfobject of Kohut (1971, 1977). This other is the other that the infant "discovers" in its relationship to the mothering other—an other who is not distant, not rule bound and with whom powerful emotions of love, fear, loss, joy, and grief are experienced. The boundaries between self and other here are fuzzy and porous. Similarly, the boundaries between imaginary and symbolic are permeable and exchanges between the two domains are fluid. Another way of saying this is that the thinking about self and other in the domain of *other-with-a-little-o* is prone to primary process thinking. In this realm, the self and other may at one moment be held in a somewhat stable manner by a symbolic representation, only to be disrupted the next moment by an influx primary process thought—subject-object reversal, condensation, displacement, metaphors that collapse into concreteness and metonymy that is then repressed.

From these last few paragraphs there emerges the notion that all discussions of alterity could be placed in these two registers, that is, they could be describing self-other (little o) or self-Other (big O). Lacan did not see these two domains as occurring in a developmental sequence. The term "register" implies synchrony or parallelism.

We can see that the concept of alterity, even when viewed from within the confines of psychology is by no means a unitary idea. It morphs and undergoes redefinition depending on the paradigm of psychology one happens to be in at the time. Most psychological paradigms (for psychology is in what Kuhn (1996) would call a preparadigmatic state) do not address this definitional problem. As we shall see, Lacan and Dabrowski do offer fruitful possibilities in this direction. Lacan because he, as we have seen, addresses the problem of the other explicitly; and Dabrowski, because his theory is a theory of theories and thus offers us a taxonomic system for all of psychology's concepts.

B: Philosophy and Alterity

The maker of all things took Union and Division, and Identity, and Alterity and Station and Motion to compleat the Soul."

Stanley, "History of Philosophy" (1701 p.377)

Almost all philosophical thought addresses the issue of alterity implicitly, and many thinkers deal with it explicitly. So broad is the array of thinkers in this domain that a thorough critical review is well beyond my capacities. Thus, all that is intended here is a brief overview of some of the major positions. The result of this survey will demonstrate considerable instability of thought in this area.

Descartes' *cogito* ("I think therefore, I am") provides a good and traditional starting place. Here, the sense of self, and by extension, of other, is founded upon thought. If one's sense of rationality is stable, then so is one's sense of self and other. However, if we introduce alternative "thinkings" (for example, primary process thinking), then we move as Ricoeur (1970, 1995) points out, to notions of self and other beyond the *cogito*. Similar destabilizing forces are introduced with the advent of romantic philosophers and philosophers who include "non-rational" (in the narrow sense of the term) concepts such as spirit or soul.

The famous Hegelian "fight to the death" between master and slave can also be understood as an explanatory parable of self and other

(Hegel, 1807). Self and other face each other at first in mortal combat. It must be one over the other. One submits, unwilling to further risk their life, and the other becomes the master. Self and other then enter a phase of one up, one down. Hegel describes how, through struggle and work, the subjugated one attains mastery and a concordance is achieved between self and other. No longer is it self versus other, or self over other. It is now self with other. Hegel and later interpreters (Kojève 1947 and Fukuyama 2006) link this to the historical inevitability of the spread of democracies, political systems where self is *with* other as in *"we the people."*

This system is modified, if not radically destabilized, with the advent of pluralistic, distributed conceptions of self and other that we find in post-modern philosophers such as Derrida (2007) and Lyotard (1984), notions that find expression in many of the ideas of Lacan, for example, in his ideas of the mirror stage and the falsifying function of the ego.

Levinas (1969, 1987, 2000, 2006) has written extensively on the topic of alterity and many of his ideas inform this study. For Levinas, the other is something beyond, beyond the self, and otherwise than being. The other beckons the self into the unknown, beyond the limits of one's own being. Furthermore, the other, insofar as it is apprehended and acknowledged, implies, Levinas argues, a prehension, a presumption of, an assumed possibility of language, of communication. Thus in this there is a paradox. The other is at once radically other, beckoning us into the beyond. The other is also automatically in communion insofar as the very perception of the other involves connection.

In, "Time and the Other," (1987) Levinas develops the argument that, "time is not the achievement of an isolated and lone subject, but that it is the very relationship of the subject with the Other" (p.39). The consequences of this assertion are indeed radical, for it places the concept of alterity in a fundamental position with regard to being. Not least of the consequences of this line of thought is a radical reformulation of Heidegger's (1927) assertions on being. Given that for Heidegger time and being are inextricably intertwined the position of the others is to a great extent relegated to the "they"…the forces of conformity. The other is not seen as the very wellspring of being, as it is in Levinas, but as a threat to authenticity. Implicit in the position that Levinas takes is a critique of much of Sartre, who regards, in much of his thought, the other as oppressive and imprisoning. For Levinas, the Other beckons to us, is mysterious and incomprehensible and leads us beyond ourselves. It calls to us inspiring self transcendence. It is this that we desire inexhaustibly. This line of thought leads us to a very different place with regard to the relationship to the other, a position that Levinas further spells out in "Totality and Infinity" (1969). Levinas offers a conceptualization of the self-other relationship that leads towards a "pluralism that does not merge into unity" (1969, p.42).

According to Levinas, the act of existing results in a tragic solitude and a materiality that besets us with needs (material needs that are different from the desire for the other mentioned above). This solitude is confronted with "the face of the other" which defines us, establishes time and history and calls us beyond ourselves. It is this Other that remains eternally mysterious. Levinas points out that this intersubjective space is vulnerable to distortions and asymmetries but implies that such asymmetries are not inevitable. Such asymmetries are perhaps part of the psychological experience of self and other, which involve emotions such as sympathy and communication. Levinas is describing a different register of self-other experience when he addresses issues of time, transcendence, totality and infinity in the relationship of the self to the other.

Levinas pushes the argument further; for death is absolutely other. Death is also always in the future, as far as being is concerned. If one *is* then death is not. If death *is* then one is not. Thus that which is futural is alteric. In this way, yet another link between time and the other is uncovered. (One cannot resist the temptations to link psychodynamic conceptions of the death instinct, the trauma of birth and alterity at this point—more of this later).

In yet another, perhaps more controversial step in his exposition, Levinas argues connections between sexuality, or voluptuousness and alterity. When he states, "the contrariety that permits its terms to remain absolutely other is the *feminine*" he introduces some provocative notions indeed, notions that have opened him up to criticisms of sexism by de Beauvoir (1993). However, if we try to rescue these statements as metaphors, perhaps or to allow for socio-cultural constructions of the feminine as other, we can perhaps retain and gain some exceedingly useful insights while generating interesting questions, such as, "To what extent has the feminine been recruited to stand for the Other, and what have been the consequences of this?"

Continuing with the related theme of sex, Levinas provokes some interesting ideas on the "caress." The caress acknowledges the other and is intimately related to time, especially to conceptions of the future. In extending his argument thus and in examining the special form of alterity that emanates from the relationship of paternity, Levinas is indeed making bold and original connections, connections that fire up yet other possibilities insofar as eroticism, voluptuousness and paternity are central concepts for Freud. After reading Levinas, we are invited to go back and re-read Freud, and ultimately to re-think our praxis in the consulting room. These issues will be addressed in Chapter II, "Clinical Applications."

Readers who are familiar with Buber's conception of "dialogue" (1958) may think that Levinas is re-stating Buber. Levinas is clear on his difference. His thought is at odds with Buber where, in his opinion, "the ineluctable character of isolated subjectivity is underestimated." It is as if Levinas wishes to acknowledge and respect the radical, tragic isolation of the subject who has, to use Tillich's (1952) felicitous term, "the courage to be."

As Wiley states in his introduction to "Totality and Infinity"(1969), the world (of philosophers) can perhaps be divided into "totalizers" (who wish to join or amalgamate all into one) and "infinitizers" (who wish to preserve radical uniqueness and alterity—along with its mystery). Parmenides is a totalizer. Levinas asserts that he wishes to provide counter-arguments to Parmenides by acknowledging the transcendent unknowableness of the other and the robustness of the ensuing isolation of the subject.

Ross-Fryer (2004) creates excellent counterpoints between Levinas' notions of alterity and Lacan's conception of self and other while also elaborating the ethical processes that result from these different subjectivities and different alterities. This counterpointing of Lacan and Levinas brings to light a dimension of differentiation that can be laid across the field of alterity. This dimension can be called essentialism versus non-essentialism. The assumption of essentialism involves the assumption that the self, and by extension the other, is focal and "exists" through time. In religious thought the notion of essentialism is connected with notions like the soul and reincarnation of essential aspects of the self. This idea resurfaces in the two broad forms of Buddhism—essentialist and non-essentialist. (Suzuki, 1956). Non-essentialism involves ideas of dispersal of or non-existence of the self (and, by extension, the other). Such ideas are found in the religion of Zen Buddhism, in the philosophy of Sartre, where the "centre" of the self is a void. It is also found, in a different form, in the ideas of Lacan where the self is visualized as a "torus," a doughnut shape, where the center of gravity exists in the hole in the middle. In this Lacan is arguing that the self is perhaps to be viewed as a holographic image existing as an imaginary construct "outside" the boundaries of the self.

Pragmatically oriented philosophers (James,1978; Dewey,1998; Rorty, 1981, 2000) would, by very definition, have a practical view of the self. Such questions as "What is the true nature of the self or other?" would only have meaning if they have practical import. The truth is what works best, that which is functional. Thus, one "walks around," "passes over," or ignores questions such as those concerning "ultimate realities" if they do not concern practical problems. Self and other are, in this philosophy, the pragmatic self and the pragmatic other. These notions may change with time and context, depending on what is functional. Thus, any of the understandings of self and other covered by all thinkers in this book and all others could be acceptable as an assertible working idea, if it meets the practical exigencies of the situation. We are very close to Wittgenstein's statement (2001), "That of which we cannot speak we must pass over in silence."

The tension between essentialist and non-essentialist conceptions of self and other shows up in the field of phenomenological philosophy. On the one hand, early writers, such as Husserl, seem to argue that, while one's approach to the object or subject should stay as close as possible to phenomena as they are to perception, eventually, through the process of reduction, one will appreciate the thing in itself, its essence. This can be understood as a clinging to earlier philosophical notions of the construction of a perfect (or near perfect) mirror of nature. In other phenomenological approaches and in pragmatic approaches such as Rorty, and even in the psychological thinking of Rogers, such essentialist/realist ideas are all but abandoned, leaving one with a constructed, contingent and thus mutable, non-essential self (and Other).

Further discriminations emerge when one asks the question, "What should one do with this self?" Nietzsche and Heidegger point with suspicion towards this constructed self, the former arguing that it should be overcome, challenged and stretched to its limits. Heidegger with concepts of the "they" and "thrownness" seems to take a more measured view of this possibility. In each case, the other can present a possibility for freedom, but is viewed as more probably being an object of suspicion, an other whose aim is to render one conformist and inauthentic. Self and other are differentiated and valued in these systems according to the extent they have constructed themselves along lines free from blind conformity or abjection.

In Merleau-Ponty (2003), we find a theme (elaborated upon by Ricoeur) where self and other are seen as determined by language. The human being is seen as being linguistic through and through. We are born into a web of language of pre-established grammars, meanings, codes, terms, lexicons, syntaxes and vocabularies. These are inescapable. We are captivated and captured by this vast linguistic system and it is this that defines our sense of self and other. We live a linguistic self and other, and if we wish to understand these phenomena, we must approach them through language. Again, Lacan, with one of his bases in Saussure (1998) the linguist, is close to this stream of thought.

The humanistic tradition has, as one of its way-stations, the work of Rousseau. One element of this tradition is the notion of the realization of the true potential of the self. This notion is usually yoked to essentialist ideas of self and other. One finds echoes of this, interestingly enough, in the early writings of Marx (1983) for whom work is seen as an opportunity, under ideal circumstances, to realize one's true self, to actualize it in reality. The concept of alienation issuing from this idea takes on a different meaning from the conventional interpretations of Marx. This meaning is closer to Marx's earlier ideas (1844, 1961) where work is understood to be the way in which humans realize themselves. Alienation from one's labor, from this perspective, is to be split off from the capacity to realize oneself through one's work. This alienation is alienation from one's true (essential) self.

Here we are very close to Maslow's notion of the self-actualized person, the person busily and actively engaged in realizing their true self. This essentialist view is often the casualty, or at least the target, of many "post humanist" or "anti-humanist" critiques (ably remarked upon by Ross-Fryer, 2004).

Ideas of true self and false self can still survive such critiques as can potentially important elements of this tradition. One way is to use the definition of false self developed by the psychoanalyst Winnicott

(1960, 1964, 1965a, b, 1971a, b) as "The part of the self erected to deal with impingements from the environment" and refrain from defining the true self except insofar as to say it is not the false self. The true self is thus left indeterminate and spontaneous, in a way, full of surprises. (I elaborate on this in *The Experience of Emptiness* [2003]). This line of thought also eludes the strong critique of Adorno in *The Jargon of Authenticity* (2006). Levinas, in honoring the self as a potential, takes a similar tack.

What all this implies for alterity is significant. Is the other viewed as being "true" or "false," in "good faith," "authentic," "ecstatic"? Is the other engaged in the process of realizing or expressing an essential, definable, true self or is she an indefinable, spontaneous unknown standing for the beyond? To what extent can we let the other be these possibilities? Can we endure these situations?

Vlastos, in his examination of Plato's conception of the cosmos (1975), implicitly alerts us to the role of observation and the desire for order. Close observation of the movement of celestial objects can make us aware that our ordered conception of the cosmos is inaccurate. We become aware, in these moments, of disconfirmation, of the alterity of the cosmos, for it stands outside our previously constructed model. At this point, we have a choice: do we allow the world to be "other" and, for a while, at least, beyond us, or do we re-assert our pre-existing world view that preserves the continuity between us and the world? Do we take on a Popperian (2002) stance and allow for disconfirmation; do we let our theories be corrigible, which is to let the world be other than us or do we narcissistically assert that we were right all along, and deny the new observations, holding on to the precious feeling of being at one with the world through our ideas? Thus it is that with the advent of new observational technologies; telescope, electron microscope, photographic devices, sound recorders, x-ray machines. New data emerge that create a crisis—a crisis on one level as described by Kuhn (1996) but that on another level is a crisis of alterity and the anguish of the sudden realization of alterity.

Romanyshin (1989) offers some fascinating ideas in this regard, to the effect that the invention of techniques for creating perspective in drawings and paintings in the renaissance by Alberti and Brunelleschi radically increased people's sense of separateness from the scenes depicted on the plane of the artwork. This increase in visual separation also is connected with a growing sense of psychological separation—of alterity—an alterity perhaps connected with the rise in the emphasis on the importance of the individual in the post-renaissance world. Prior to the invention of perspective all the elements in the painting occurred on the same surface and this had the effect of pulling the viewer into that same plane, in effect de-differentiating him or her. This situation reverses with the advent of perspective.

Romanyshin's argument is parallel to McLuhan who argues that the invention of moveable type at about the same time as the invention of perspective drawing, created the "Gutenberg Galaxy," namely an alteration in the sensorium such that there was a separation between the reader and the medium. Print is a "hot" medium—a medium that disjoints and disrupts feelings of universal participation. Face to face, spoken media and television, are "cool" media—media that facilitate a sense of global participation. In the television age this sense of participation brought on by the medium of television gives rise to the phenomenon of the "global village." These examples provide provocative ideas as to how technologies can profoundly affect conceptions of alterity and in so doing, of course, dramatically influence all other spheres of sociality; politics, religion, art, families, ethics, economics.

Ricoeur (1992) carries out ten studies of "ipseity" (selfhood) and alterity (otherness) offering a multifaceted approach to the fundamental philosophical problem of the self and other. In a sequence of ten studies, the issue of self and other is examined from a semantic, pragmatic, agentic, narrative, ethical, practical and ontological approach. It is a dense, challenging and rewarding read.

Ricoeur has three intentions in this work. First, he argues for the "primacy of reflective meditations over the immediate positing of the subject." In this Ricoeur would seem to be arguing for a primary focus on the phenomenology of self and other as opposed to, say, Cartesian assertions that lead to positions on self and other arrived at through rational exertions. Second, Ricoeur hopes to distinguish between "self" and "identity." Both concepts are related to time, with a temporality that is often involved in narratives. Third, Ricoeur wishes to establish a dialectic between self and other than self, an "otherness of a kind that can be constitutive of selfhood as such." This would seem to be a dialectic in which the self finds itself in a confrontation with the other. Using concepts that have a distinctly Hegelian ring, Ricoeur aims to show that one cannot be thought of without the other, thus the title of his book, *Oneself as Another*.

Ricouer argues that the *cogito* of Descartes is vulnerable to a Nietszchean attack since the "I….is an interpretation of a causal type." The "I" of Descartes which is arrived at through a process of reduction or elimination until one discovers that which is foundational is more correctly understood as a polymorphous result of a hermeneutics of the self. The "I" is a result more of interpretation than causation.

It is this interpretative process, in all its complexity that Ricoeur spells out in the remainder of the text. The "I" is thus posited (with its inevitable alteric counterpart) in the philosophy of language, action, narrative and time, ethics and morality. This series of studies, which Ricoeur admits to be fragmentary, challenges the simplicity of the *cogito*. "Who?" emerges as an arduous problem.

Jacques Derrida, in "Psyche: Invention of the Other" (2007), offers yet further perspectives, ideas and associations on the concept of the Other. These ideas come from his "deconstructionist" viewpoint, but, as we shall see, have fascinating overlaps and potentials for correspondence with other ideas in this field.

First, Derrida connects the concept of otherness with that of invention. An invention, if it is a true invention (for many things are labeled as inventions that are merely re-hashings of the old) involves some illegality, a going beyond the rules. Thus an invention, paradoxically is the creation of the impossible. An invention must also be *countersigned* as in a patent or a *brevet*. This countersigning means that the *other* is a necessary component for the invention to take place. An invention also "ought to introduce a disordering mechanism." It disrupts the *status quo* since an invention finds something for the very first time. Derrida casts suspicion upon programs for invention. How can such unexpectedness, such impossibility be programmed? To be programmed is to be expected.

Combining these thoughts, Derrida arrives at the following:

> *"The aleatory advent of the entirely other- beyond the incalculable as still possible calculus - there is "true" invention which is no longer invention of truth and can only come about for a finite being: the very opportunity (chance) of finitude: It invents and appears to itself only on the basis of what happens thus." (2007, p. 418)*

In this Derrida appears very close to Levinas insofar as the other is posited as that incalculable that exists beyond. Its beyondness implies our finitude and at the same time reminds us of our finitude while inviting us further into the incalculable. As soon as the other becomes calculable, it is no longer an other, but has fallen under the rubric of the subject.

Further associations of this concept include the following. Jean Badiou (2005) in his examination of the idea of an event leads us close to the concept of an invention, which is an event—an event which takes us beyond ourselves. Bion, in his examination of "wild thoughts" (1997) is very close to Derrida's ideas about invention and the other, for with Derrida, the other occurs as a wild thought. Bion reminds us that we have varying needs and capacities to tame wild thoughts. We thus have varying capacities to tolerate radical alterity. And finally this alterity that Derrida explicates, or reveals, is close to Lacan's *jouissance* (1977) or the "accursed share" of Bataille (1991). The other is too much to bear. We recoil, constrict, retract our sensorium, or (as with Bataille) we must destroy this excess, this surplus, perhaps ceremonially.

Derrida argues that this concept of other rehabilitates the "transcendental imagination or the productive imagination from Kant to Schelling and Hegel." In so doing it seems to inflate the spirit. In this regard we can see that Derrida's thoughts have lead to a position that is somewhat countercultural in those groups that are dominated by rational pragmatism. "The other is not the possible." insists Derrida, this conclusion emanating from the preceding deconstructive efforts. The possible is not truly new. The truly new is impossible. The other, to be truly new in its alterity, must be impossible. "The other is indeed what is not inventable, and it is therefore the only invention in the world, the only invention of the world, *our* invention, the invention that invents *us*. For the other is always another origin of the world and *we are to be invented*." (p.45) Derrida reminds us that, "The other is not the new." For the "new" is that which is conceived in our present paradigm. The other, the radically other, does not exist in these terms. Finally Derrida states, "The call of the other is a call to come, and that happens only in multiple voices." This last leaves his thought open, but perhaps what is being pointed to here is that the openness to radical alterity is a willingness to hear multiple voices, to hear a call in many registers, tones and timbres. Again, clear harmonies with Levinas are to be discerned here.

What then, of the famous quote from Sartre, namely, "Hell is Other People"? Hell is in the experiencing of the other, especially the other saturated with desire. We desire them, but they can never fulfill our desire. They desire us and we eternally frustrate them as we are also imprisoned by their desire for us. It is as if their desire for us prevents them from seeing us as we are and as an end in ourselves. Sartre locates his drama "Huis Clos" (No Exit, 1987) in another place, but it seems he is saying the condition that obtains in his drama is a universal one.

It is as if Sartre is dramatizing a possible differentiation between Lacan's *desire* and *demand*.

Desire is the ineffable obscure, never-ending wish (akin to Freud's *wunsch*). Reading Lacan, it is as if desire is left conceptually in a protean undifferentiated state, prior to the emergence of objects of desire, targets, aims; prior to the qualities of desire. Desire for Lacan is pure desire—desire in itself.

Demand on the other hand, is a derivative of desire. Demand has specificity. It has qualities, properties, aims, targets and states. Demand can be named: sex, wholeness, money, recognition, food, defecation, a person.

Even though a demand may be, to all interests and purposes, met, ineffable desire is left externally wanting. Yet, demands are seductive in their pull. We eternally seek satisfaction in the demands we place on the world, only to be eternally frustrated because desire is by its very definition insatiable through the realization of demands.

This formulation gives a different slant to Freud's statement that one ends a course of analysis "sadder but wiser." Ordinarily the sadness is associated with the analysand's awareness that they have repressed memories that cost them their freedom. From this perspective, however, the sadness has to do with the Sisyphean struggle to quench desire with demands, coupled with the realization both of the hopelessness and the inevitability of this situation.

Again we find an array of definitions and understandings of the concept of alterity in the field of philosophy. However, the concept of alterity does at least exist as a concept in the field of philosophy.

One can find the word in dictionaries of philosophy. This leads to a rich thinking on and around the topic—thinking that would be of considerable benefit to psychology if it were to be entertained for a while. However, it appears that psychology, the child of philosophy, has been overly eager to establish its difference from its parent and its other siblings, for example, anthropology and sociology. This adolescent leaving of home has resulted in an unfortunate impoverishment of the field, especially in recent decades. I believe much is to be gained by psychology using concepts from neighboring fields and subjecting them to the methodologies unique to it. Psychology is old enough that it may re-visit its birthplace without losing its identity.

C: Religion and Alterity

"In the Trinity there is, 1. Ipseity; 2. Alterity; 3. Community."

Coleridge, *"Notes from the Table Talk." (1827)*

"Meu coracao vagabundo quer guarda o mundo em mim."

Caetano Veloso, *"Coracao Vagabundo"*

In the field of religion we find a spectrum of notions of self and other. On the one hand, narratives and precepts seem based on conventional, legalistic notions of self and other. Here, the self is separate from the other and one is responsible only for one's own behavior. On the other hand, we find many religious writings with notions of the self and other that are quite different. In these writings the conventional schema of self and other is held to be an illusion. This illusion is supplanted by other notions of self and other, notions that one typically finds at the mystical core of many religions, notions that often bear a great resemblance to one another.

One set of notions that differ from conventional notions of alterity involve the realization of self-other identity or fusion. This is captured in the Sanskrit epithet "Tat Twam asi" (Thou art that), (cited in Ouspensky, 1998) implying that self and other are the same, or interchangeable, that the idea of separateness is false. This idea is given poetic form by John Donne in his famous sermon in which he asserts, "no man is an island, each one is part of the main." In this, Donne (1624) is echoing the early English Christian mystics who felt that approaching God involved a dissolution of the self, a going into a "cloud of unknowing."

In turn, this is similar to notions of the self found in the Upanishads of early Hindu scripture (1997). Here, it appears that even the term "self" means not the isolated individual but *atman*, or the "oversoul" which can be very loosely read as "all selves." The poetry of Sufism (Shah, 1991), which can be regarded as a mystical element of Islam, sometimes using the metaphorical vehicle of the love relationship, or of madness, captures the experience of loss of self in the other, other in self.

Similar ideas can be found in Gnostic teachings, (especially in the concept of the Pleroma) and it is indeed interesting that C.G. Jung, one of the few psychologists to integrate alternative views of self and other into his theory, has arguably been deeply influenced by Gnostic writings (Hoeller, 1989). Zen Buddhism provides a different response to the space left behind when one asserts that conventional notions of self and other are illusory. While other religions provide the notion of self-other identity or fusion, Zen offers nothingness, void. Ideas of self-other identity still preserve residual ideas of "self" and "other." Zen allows none of this. Here we encounter the dilemma between *essentialist* and *non-essentialist* notions of self (and thus, by extension, of other). The Zen approach is that of non-essentialism. In a manner close (at least at first sight) to Sartre (1956), it is argued that the self has no essence, "coalesces" around nothingness, that the very notion of existence is an illusion, a falsification of the ego. This is also interestingly similar to the "Torus" of Lacan (1977). If there is no self and no other, only nothingness, then there can be no fusion of self and other. There is, to allude to yet another religion, only Tao, a paradoxical totality and nothingness.

In these two religious responses to the issue of alterity, namely a response which holds a sacred, deep connectedness with the other who yet remains other and the response that views the very notions of self and other as a falsification, an illusion, we find an interesting parallel with the views, respectively of Levinas and Lacan. The counterpoints of these two approaches and the ethical stances issuing therefrom have been examined by Ross-Fryer (2004). In this, we find contact points between religion, philosophy and psychology. In Chapter V of this book, the theory of positive disintegration (Dabrowski 1970. 1977) is used as a framework to integrate ideas across this field.

D: Social Science and Alterity

"True scientific knowledge, on the contrary, demands abandonment to the very life of the object."

Hegel,
The Phenomenology of Mind (1807)

"All mysterious misfortune is alteric."

Taussig,
Mimesis and Alterity (1992)

"Alienation is essentially experiencing the world and oneself passively, receptively, as the subject separated from the object."

Fromm (1961, p.44)

As mentioned at the outset, while psychology dictionaries do not contain the term "alterity" the same is not true of the lexicon of the related social sciences. In these, the concept is utilized broadly and deeply. The following sample gives a sense of the breadth and depth of these approaches in the fields of anthropology, sociology, cultural studies and political science.

If we apply the theory propounded by Berger and Luckmann (1991) we arrive at the notion that the very concept of alterity is a social construction and, as such, is subject to the forces involved in the sociology of knowledge. The meanings of alterity will be shaped by social forces, forces that, through various means, gain and maintain their legitimacy in universes of discourse. Implicit in this approach is a critical attitude toward the very concept, an asking of the question: "To what ends and by what means do we have these conceptions of alterity?" Such an approach is redolent with ideas from critical theory, Marx, Freud and Nietzsche. It is such an approach that is somewhat lacking in the field of psychology.

Marx (1844, 1961) identifies two forms of alienation in the worker. The first and most widely-known form is the sense of alienation from the means of production. The second, and perhaps more important meaning, the meaning usually overlooked in analyses and applications of Marx's ideas, (Fromm (1961) being a notable exception) is the type of alienation the worker has when work is not felt to be a vehicle for self realization. It is in this second meaning that Marx comes very close in his thinking to humanist thinkers found in the capitalist world; for example, Maslow's and Rogers' concepts of the "self actualizing person"(1968) and the "fully functioning person"(1961).

Marx "is concerned with the liberation of man from the kind of work which destroys his individuality, which transforms him into a thing, and which makes him a slave of things" (Fromm, 1961, p 48-49). This type of alienated work not only splits a person from his labor but also separates him or her from others and from the human race as a whole. Marx thus argues that there is a connection between the nature of work, the means of production and the ways in which we experience others. There is a connection between work and alterity. If our labor is alienated, that is to say, if we do not find ourselves and develop our fullest potential through our work, then we are split off from ourselves, the means of production and from others—split off from others in an immediate, one-on-one sense of our interpersonal relationships with others and also split off from our *"species being,"* our sense of being united with all humanity. Thus Marx is placing the conventional sense of alterity, with its inherent notions of separateness, isolation and individualism as a direct result of exploitative, alienated labor.

Taussig, in *Mimesis and Alterity*, offers a dazzling array of ideas on the sense of otherness, relating it, among other things, to Frazer's ideas of magic (2006). When we confront the other and feel some threat from it we attempt to gain control over it through the magic of contact and imitation. In these, we attempt to negate the object's otherness by gaining contact with it through its appurtenances, or by imitating it (through mimesis). We become the object and thus gain control of it.

Thus, those who have been colonized, subjugated by a colonial other, will, paradoxically at first blush, mimic the colonizer, in a manner close to Freud's notion of "identification with the aggressor," and parallel to dynamics Fanon depicts in *Black Faces, White Masks* (2008). However, Taussig seems to assert that this seeming fusion with the object is not always complete. At times, we note "mimetic excess" as, for example, in the film depicting case of "Trobriand Cricket" (1976) where the Trobrianders take up the English game of cricket, integrating into it aspects built on imitations of occupying Australian forces in World War II and elements of their non-colonized lifestyles. Thus, "mimesis plays this trick of dancing between the same and the very different." (Taussig, 1992, p. 129) In addition, sometimes this mimesis is an attempt "to simulate an imagined savagery in order to dominate or destroy it." (p. 80) This dynamic is parallel to the process of introjection of the "bad object" described by Fairbairn (1952).

Alterity: The Experience of the Other

Thus, Taussig yokes mimesis to alterity and control of the other. From this we may see instances where there is competition over who is gaining the power accruing from effective mimesis. Similarly, we may observe instances where there is specialization over the "task" of mimesis, certain subgroups or individuals take up the task of imitation.

Taussig observes the not infrequent phenomenon amongst colonized peoples where the men imitate the colonizers while the women retain traditional dress. In addition, the colonized will adorn themselves in "colonialized alterity…European symbols of Indianness." It is as if a collusive agreement exists between colonizer and colonized as to how the alterity should be registered and manifested and how much it may be consciously experienced.

This dynamic is related to the experience of the uncanny and here, Taussig imports Freud's ideas. The uncanny is the return of the repressed familiar. That which was once familiar (non-alteric) is repressed and when it returns later is experienced as a bizarre mixture of familiar and strange—the uncanny.

Taussig indeed offers a different vertex from which to view the phenomenon of alterity. Several hypotheses or suspicions emerge. First, that while many psychologists posit a developmental thrust towards separation-individuation, there is arguably a thrust in humans to become one with the other, not only as a regression to symbiosis but as part and parcel of a wish to control the other, to reduce its alterity and thus the extent to which it may take us by surprise. Secondly, while some psychologists speak of the capacity of "oceanic experience" or the capacity to identify with the other as a marker of a high level of psychological development, we should perhaps regard this assertion with a similar level of suspicion.

Perhaps this capacity to feel at one with the world or even the universe is a magical attempt at gaining control over that which is other.

Jean Baudrillard and Marc Guillaume in "Radical Alterity" (2008) examine the phenomenon of alterity as it manifests itself in society from multiple perspectives. It seems as if Baudrillard and Guillaume have taken several of the ideas of Levinas and Derrida and applied them to concrete observable phenomena in the world.

Their description of the phenomenon of radical alterity seems close to that of Levinas and to the notion of *differance* in Derrida (2007). "Absolute singularity is a unique sign with no relation to the general and no possibility of exchange" (Baudrillard and Guillaume, 2007, p. 18) And again, "absolute alterity is unthinkable" (p.25). On the other hand they observe many phenomena in society that lead them to the conclusion that, "alterity is in danger" (p.113).

Many forces, often driven by technology, put this form of radical alterity at risk. The great age of exploration of distant lands is over. It is uncommon for us to meet a person from a culture that is radically different from ours, with whom we do not share a television program or a pop song or an item of clothing. In response to this decline of "geographical exoticism" they note the creation of "artificial strangeness," especially in urban societies. Individuals are resorting more to "interior alterity" where they explore internal "selves" or identities as a means of substituting for the lost experience of the other. At the same time, Baudrillard and Guillaume challenge whether, even during the great explorations there was a true experience of alterity. Since, for the most part, what we see is the creation of a "fiction of the other"…a fiction that is based upon subjective factors such that the other is not experienced as truly alteric, but as an extension of the subject.

They also note that today alterity is managed by "bureaucrats of alterity" such as doctors and psychiatrists. One could possibly add to that most diversity programs or attempts at cultural understanding that do not include conceptions of radical alterity.

In addition they argue that there is a new form of sociality emerging as radical alterity declines—a form of sociality that is "spectral," Here they play on the multiple meanings of the word "spectral"—ghostly, and prismatic, "today's sociality is based on a generalized 'relationalism' rather than anomic individualism." This is indeed a telling point, for what they are arguing here is that the anomie described by, say, Durkheim (1951) and characteristic of industrial society, has been replaced by a ghostly dispersed form of "connectedness" in the post modern era. The cautionary note is a subtle but important one. We may be fooled or seduced into believing we are related to "others" while the underlying anomie remains and we have lost the transcendence of the radically other. We may end up losing both connectedness and alterity in the postmodern era and in the "complete artificialization of the world" (2008. p.113). Baudrillard and Guillaume argue, "We are not trying to create a world of conciliation and recognition," this just leads back to the same thing and destroys the all-important phenomenon of radical alterity. In several ways the criticism of the homogenization of the world in the post-modern era is a familiar one. However in importing the idea of radical alterity (it seems from Levinas and Derrida) a possible solution seems to be offered. It is important to preserve the true, ineluctable mystery of the Other, despite technologies, despite the massive seductive processes operating so powerfully and omnipresently, despite regularization involved in ever-expanding bureaucracies, and despite resistances in ourselves.

Anna Kerttula (2000) portrays the tensions and interactions among three cultural groups on the Chukotka Peninsula at the northeastern tip of what used to be the USSR. The Yupik hunt sea mammals; the Chukchi herd reindeer on the tundra and the newcomers, who immigrated from the west of the USSR, occupy positions in management, education and politics. Kerttula shows how each group sustains its identity by "othering" the other two groups and how, while this is based on very different routines of production and places of production (sea, tundra, village), it is furthered through the use of symbols (antlers, blubber, boats, vodka) and though cultural activities (marriage patterns, gifts, beliefs, rituals, entertainment, education). Kerttula also demonstrates how larger scale political changes (for example, the rise and fall of the USSR) and technological changes (snowmobiles, trucks, television, films) can radically impact the sense of otherness at this cultural level.

Carrier in "De los Otros" (1995) examines homosexuality in males in Western Mexico. The title of this work itself indicates the topic of alterity, "Of the Others," There is much of interest in this text. Of note to our present study are two features. First, there is the delicacy with which the otherness of being gay in Mexico is handled by the families of those he studies. Carrier is studying a culture that values both a cohesive family and heterosexuality highly. Carrier would note that as it becomes more and more "obvious" that a male family member is gay (for example, he had not married and is getting older) he would become subject to much teasing and joking regarding his sexual orientation. It was as if his otherness was half acknowledged, half hidden in this ribald humor, as if the alterity was "solved" in a compromise formation of humor that attempted to meet both the values of family cohesion and heterosexuality.

A second point of note in the nomenclature of homosexuality seems apposite. Carrier notes that the categorization of gayness is different from that ordinarily found in, say, the USA. "Activo" describes a man who plays the active, insertive role in the homosexual act. This is not regarded as "gay"; it is more likely to be regarded as the behavior of a highly sexed man. "Passivo" denotes the male who is in the passive, receptive role in the sex act, and this is categorized as "gay" or "ambiente." "Internationale" designates the individual who is willing to take up either an "activo" or "passivo" role. Carrier cites evidence to support the notion that there is considerable importance attached to these designations, that there is risk in misidentifying others as say, "passivo" when they are "activo."

What does this mean in terms of our present study? It indicates that cultures have, at times, to wrestle with this phenomenon of alterity since it can in some formulations conflict with other vital cultural values (family, equality, heterosexuality) and that social mores (everyday comportment, jokes) and category systems (language, taxonomic systems, even diagnoses) can be and are altered, tinkered with, welded, even radically transformed so as to adjust the othering of others.

Marshall McLuhan's works (1962, 2003, 2005) as mentioned earlier, offer interesting connections between the experience of otherness and technology, especially technologies of communication. The medium of television, a "cool" medium, he argues, is an intensely, overwhelmingly participatory one. It breaks down barriers of space and time and recreates the sense of oneness one could imagine existing around a campfire tens of thousands of years ago. Television alters the whole sensorium of the viewer. So radical is this alteration that he argues that what is on the television is not as important as the deep change that takes place in the sensorium of the viewer.

Print, on the other hand, is a "hot" medium. Print is linear and emphasizes subject-object differentiation. When we read a newspaper, for example, it is not like a face-to-face encounter, not like television where much information is taken in simultaneously and participation in and with the other is maximized. When we read a newspaper we keep a certain distance from the object and we take in information sequentially, one step, word or phrase at a time.

Thus technology alters the sense of alterity, and doing so alters all elements of society, including politics, ideas, ethics, economics and social structures.

Several ideas from the corpus of critical theory bear upon the topic of alterity. Marcuse's notion of "one dimensional man" (1964) is provocative in its implications insofar as it could be argued that the one dimensionality of consciousness apparent in post industrial society is indicative of an eradication of the sense of alterity, that through such mechanisms of *repressive desublimation* and *repressive tolerance,* the sense of alienation has been, to a great extent, foreclosed. The consequences of this for personal and social change are, in Marcuse's opinion, indeed serious.

We thus find in the domain of the social sciences a vigorous and interesting approach to the topic of alterity where it is linked to ideas of trauma, colonialism, deviance and social difference. It is often the case that psychology has more to learn from the social sciences than vice versa, and this situation seems to obtain with regard to the concept at hand.

E: Art and Alterity

"Je est un autre."

Rimbaud(2008)

"…of all the senses, that of smell, which is attracted without objectifying—bears clearest witness to the urge to lose oneself in and become the "other".

Horkheimer and Adorno, "The Dialectic of Enlightenment"(2002)

The theme of alterity is prominent in many works of art in many modalities. Following are some examples from film, novels and the visual arts to show how art and artists have addressed the complexity of this domain.

The work of Samuel Beckett (1958, 1966) is full of references to experiences of self and other. In one of his most desolate short stories, two "minimal" persons Bim and Bom encounter one another in an endless expanse of mud. Slowly, painstakingly they come to recognize and name each other.

Kafka's "Metamorphosis" (2006) can be seen as dealing with a radical otherness of the self and how, when this radical *other–that–is–self* is encountered by *others-as–self*, it is treated by them as an alien, disgusting sub human – a cockroach.

Nabokov's, "Invitation to an Execution" (1989) provides an exquisite rendering of "others" who visit, cajole, torment, imprison and even threaten to execute. In the *denouement* these others are revealed as self-parts, the whole narrative being revealed as an interior dialogue made external. This is interestingly reminiscent of the oft-repeated comforting words of the guide in the Tibetan book of the dead, exhorting us to, "Fear not, oh noble one" and reminding us that the "angry gods" are only in our minds (are only as the psychoanalyst might say, angry introjects).

Double selves, doppelgangers and multiplicities are often used as means of exploring alterities. The movie "The Double Life of Veronique" (2006), the story of Dr. Jekyll and Mr. Hyde (Stevenson, 2002) are but two examples of this genre that explores the theme of the *other–that-is-oneself* (in the former) and the *self-that-is-an-other* (in the latter case).

Poe's "William Wilson" (2003) is a short story that can be understood as a parable of alterity, remarkable, like so much of Poe, in the way it anticipates so many modern and post-modern themes. The circuitous anomalies of *the-other- that-is-self-and-other* are so deftly depicted it is small wonder that Lacan (1993) devotes so much time in his seminars to Poe. In this tale, the other/self also functions as a conscience, saboteur, and, as we discover in the *denouement*, the life force itself. This story, insofar as it links alterity with the theme of the double, alerts us to Ranks writings on this topic (1941) where tales of the *doppelganger* relate to disturbances in relation to the soul, immortality, being and death.

The song "Synchronicity" (The Police, 1983) explores alterity from a Jungian standpoint. The verses juxtapose two realities; the everyday humdrum suburban nightmare and a monster emerging from the slime of a dark Scottish loch. Implicitly there is a link between the two—the two, the suburban man and the stirring monster are, at a deeper level, one.

Adolescence can be viewed as a period when repressed selves return to the conscious mind (perhaps borne up from the depths) by the "carrier wave" of increased libido. Many works of art, especially novels and movies, elaborate on the altered alterities that emerge as a result of this identity phase-shift. Salinger's Holden Caulfield, in "Catcher in the Rye" (2001) experiences these anxiety-saturated states of otherness as he navigates, with excruciating sensitivity, his relationships and adolescent transitions.

Related to this tradition of art is the narrative of escape from a constricting self that involves encounters with that which is radically other, but a radical other that activates a fresh self. Countless romantic comedies are built upon this formula ("Pretty Woman," "Pygmalion," "Along came Polly") as are multiple narratives of adolescence, escape and travel ("On the Road," "Risky Business," "Ferris Bueller's Day Off," "Bill and Ted's Excellent Adventure").

Otherness as it is experienced in sex (either in the alterity of one's own sexuality, its own alienation from other parts of the self, or as the alterity of the body of the other in the sexual encounter) is found as a theme in art works dealing with sexuality in varying degrees of explicitness. Among the more explicit works we find "Tropic of Cancer" (1994) and many other works by Henry Miller. The reader is confronted with the otherness of the sex in the text and at the same time experiences vicariously the alterities of the narrator, for example, his astonishment at having sex with an "Egyptian woman," at making erotic contact with the exotic, the palpably other. We re-experience the transformative power and the *jouissance* of contact with the radically other.

Pornography can be understood as an art form that short-circuits this process. Instead of sustaining the alterity in the sexual encounter, it collapses self and other into a regressed narcissistic unity. The other in pornography is an ersatz other, an other that still falls inside the narcissistic orbit of self. It offers no real surprises; when it does, it can often be profoundly disruptive of the viewer's pleasures.

In another genre of art, alterity is explored via the rendition of radically different self-states. Examples of these forms would include "Fear and Loathing in Las Vegas," Edward Munch's "The Scream," Picasso's "Les Desmoisselles d'Avignon," The Beatles' "Strawberry Fields" and The Byrds' "Eight Miles High." These altered self-states are experienced as *others-that–are-self* by the protagonists and probably, in addition, as *others- that- are- other* by the audience or viewers.

"The Others" (2001), the film directed by Amenabar, recapitulates this shift from assumed self-other continuity or contiguity to radical, traumatic alterity. This movie captures the "spooky," "eerie" or uncanny feeling that can often accompany the experience and shock of radical alterity. As such, it offers a plausible explanation for the dynamics of paranoia. In this movie a mother is with her children in an isolated house on a foggy island in the English Channel. There are servants. The father is away at the war and the mother, children and servants live in isolation. In the denouement (which I will not share, so as not to "spoil" the movie for the reader) the mother and children are brought face to face with radical alterity. They encounter "the others," and in so doing must completely overhaul their view of their situation. Concurrently, memories and the history of their situation are revealed. The encounter with "the others" is a psychological catastrophe. The denial of "the others" serves to obliterate painful history.

"Fat Girl" (2004) and "A Talking Picture" (2004); are similarly structured movies insofar as they explore the phenomenon of tragic, radical alterity. In "Fat Girl" we have tension, anxiety, depression and sexuality explored in a vacationing family in the south of France. In "A Talking Picture", we see a mother and daughter visiting historical sites around the Mediterranean on a leisurely trip to meet the father in India. Both movies end suddenly and catastrophically, as something enters the narrative from "left field," from outside the narrative and we, in the audience, are shocked and traumatized by this intrusion, this radical alterity.

At first blush, these movies are reminiscent of young children's early attempts at story-writing:- "Once upon a time, there was a mommy and daddy and a baby…and then a bomb exploded, and they all died." Perhaps this story structure is not just a child's easy way of ending the story, but is actually a depiction of a meaningful structure for children—the experience of radical alterity, the radical othering that has occurred in their lives. Although I have no data to support this, this story structure is more common for boys than girls. This I would attribute to the "double othering" experienced by boys as they are so often vigorously gendered at approximately the age of three, this gendered othering having profound effects on personality and relationships throughout life. (Chodorow, 1989)

Arguably, all of these examples can fit into the scheme described in Chapter V of this text. For example, pornography would match with alterity as it is experienced at very low levels of Dabrowski's scheme while notions of synchronicity would fit with the higher levels. Genres that deal with the ubiquity of *other-as-self* and *self-that-is-other* could be seen as grappling with the intermediate levels of alterity as outlined in the scheme in Chapter V.

F: The Physiology of Alterity

"La ou ca etait, le je doit etre"

Freud (1946)

Interesting developments in the field of neurology and psychology demonstrate that the concept of alterity probably has a physiological component. Zimmer (2005) summarizes and synthesizes results from several studies that demonstrate the existence, for example, of "mirror neurons," nerve cells that fire and cause us to experience that which the other is experiencing. As an example, he cites the example of C, a 41-year-old woman in whom "the sight of someone being touched made C feel as if someone were touching her in the same place on her own body. She thought everyone had that experience." (Zimmer 2005, p. 95) Further explorations of this theme are engagingly described in Iacoboni (2008).

Further investigation showed that C had higher levels of activity in the anterior insula, an area also involved in the formation of personal memories, memories that often go toward the formation of personal identity.

Zimmer concludes that subject C was simply making an error in her anterior insula with regard to the assignment of perceptions to self or other. Since our knowledge in the field of alterity is still unstable, calling this an "outright error" is perhaps premature.

Other brain regions involved in the designation of self, and thus of other, are the precuneus which "is involved in retrieving autobiographical memories," and the medial prefrontal cortex which "may draw together perceptions and memories of self and combine them into an ongoing feeling of being oneself." (Zimmer 2005, 98) Physical alterations in these structures could result in alterations in the experience of alterity.

Much has been written on the topic of autism. This condition, which involves "a reduced ability to understand the emotions of others and a reduced capacity for social interaction and communication" (Pinel, 2007) can be understood as a constellation of behaviors indicating certain patterns in the development and deployment of the sense of alterity. This autistic situation is extremely heterogeneous and has adhering to it a panoply of explanations, some psychogenic, some physiologically based. That there may be a neurological component is indicated by the fact that autism is frequently diagnosed amongst offspring of mothers who took thalidomide during gestation. In addition, Rodier (2000) has found some indications that those diagnosed with autism sometimes have a shortened brainstem, an undeveloped facial nucleus and no superior olive, this being connected perhaps with the Hoxa 1 gene. Additional observations that those diagnosed with autism frequently have a distinctively shaped earlobe tend towards a hypothesis that the physiological events that might lead to the diagnosis of autism occur at roughly the same time as the formation of the earlobes, perhaps 20 – 24 days after conception. Autism is, at the time of this writing still a mystery, and while neurological research is advancing, the project of unifying the psychological and the physiological (Freud's grand "project") is still far from being realized.

At what may be considered an even deeper and more complex level, alterity is managed by the operations of the immune system which has structures for identifying that which is self and that which is other and that which is a potentially harmful other. The interaction of ideas, expectations, moods, emotions and cognitions with the immune system is an area of recent research in the field of psychoneuroimmunology. An excellent review of this vital and expanding domain can be found in the work of Daruna (2004).

The citing of such positivistic, materialistic findings in no way weakens the more idealistic assertions found elsewhere in this study of alterity. In Chapter V, where the theory of positive disintegration is used as an organizing template, the many different forms of alterity can be organized under one rubric that has the sense of alterity moving from simpler forms to more complex forms. The movement from simplicity to complexity is a movement that is perfectly in harmony with much of what we assume about human neurobiology.

Chapter II
Alterity: Clinical Applications

Eu nao sou eu nem sou outro
Sou qualqier coisa de intermedio:
Pilar de ponte de tedio
Que vai de mim para o Outro.

I am neither I nor other
I am somewhat intermedium:
A post of the bridge of tedium
Which runs from me to the Other.

Mario de Sa Carneiro (1890 – 1915)

A: Alterity and Psychotherapy

Much work remains to be done in this domain. Apart from Hartmann's work (1991) referred to in this text, little or no empirical investigation has been published. It would appear that the integration of a fuller understanding of the concept of alterity into the practice and dynamics of psychotherapy would result in a considerable overhauling of much current thinking and practices. Among the required adjustments in thinking would be changes involving the totalizing theories of psychotherapy and psychopathology, especially those that adhere to hard and fast diagnostic nomenclature and those that minimize the phenomenology of the client.

Parsons (2007) argues that the integration of the concept of alterity as conceived by Levinas (1969, 1987, 2000, 2006) will lead to a "different model of psychotherapy" since this integration will involve a "challenging of totalizing assumptions" and "a rejection of ontology as foundational." We encounter the other in an essentially relational manner and with a deep sense of mystery for "the other is not the sum of one's cognitive constructions." The other always lies beyond, is always transcendent.

Such psychotherapy resists diagnostic categories because, "the person who faces us is irreducible to categories, generalizations or essences." And furthermore, "a universalizing tendency can generate violence." The resistance of this universalizing tendency is ethical insofar as it preserves the "embodied mystery" of the other. The therapist conducting this type of therapy must learn "to be open to the other" and "learn to see them as a mystery." "The client is radically other, different, and speech, which utilizes categories, must be regarded with suspicion; speech proceeds from absolute difference". Finally, Parsons links this relationship to the relationship to God. Thus the encounter with the other is transcendent.

Correia (2005) attacking a similar problem, namely the impact of Levinas' thinking on psychotherapy, draws similar conclusions to Parsons (2007). The client, in his or her alterity, presents a challenge to the psychotherapist's, "pretensions of omniscience," a challenge to the tendency of the psychotherapist to reduce,"the other to a system of theoretical understanding." However, "the simple appearance of the face of the Other immediately reveals his infinite transcendence." This Other is, "pure enigma." This ineluctable enigma creates a "height" and a "misery" simultaneously in both participants. For a fully ethical encounter, both of these must be embraced. "The subject always escapes being apprehended by the therapist," and this mystery creates "height" (transcendence/beyondness) and "misery" (bereftness/unknowingness). Typically, argues Correia, this alterity is regarded as a hindrance, as something that should be eradicated, but it need not be so. One can approach psychotherapy with, "respect for the infinite of the Other."

Harris (2006) in an article discussing the course of psychotherapy undergone by T. S. Eliot in Lausanne, refers to the emergence of the other in the unconscious of the artist, "the inner other that engenders poetic language." This sense of alterity, "causes the modern poet to experience his intellect as disintegrate(ing)." As the inner other is revealed, the individual experiences, "the alterity of 'gibbering shades'." The therapeutic process, by uncovering the inner others, disrupts previous identities, and as this occurs, so one's experience of others is transmuted.

The upshot of these conclusions for the psychotherapeutic process is both subtle and dramatic. Included in a list of prescriptions emanating from these studies would seem to be the following:

> A reverence for the Otherness of the Other.
>
> Accepting the mystery of the other.
>
> Letting the Otherness of the Other pull you beyond yourself.
>
> Mistrusting diagnostic categories, theories and explanations.
>
> Mistrusting tendencies towards totalization.
>
> Suspicion of the capacity of language's capacity to capture self, Other and Relatedness.
>
> Suspicion of explanations of self and other that are "essentialistic" in nature.
>
> Openness to surprises from Self and Other, to develop the "negative capability" of Keats.

Levinas' conception of alterity, as argued elsewhere in this book, is of a high order of complexity. It is consistent with the higher levels of development that we find in Dabrowski's scheme and it is consistent with much of Lacan's work. It presents a robust and invigorating challenge, in my opinion, to much current psychotherapeutic practice.

Since all trauma is alteric and, arguably, all therapy deals with some form of trauma, all therapy deals with issues of alterity. Thus, in seeking clinical examples of alterity, alterity in the consulting room, as it were, one suffers an embarrassment of riches. Where to start?

In some ways the entire therapeutic project can be conceived of as a reformulation of alterity. In working through the transference the "other" of the therapist is liberated from the *meconaissance* of the client. The client comes to see the therapist as radically other, rather than as a puppet playing a part in the internal phantasmagoria of the client's past. The same applies to the working through of the countertransference. In a reverse flow, the client, as s/he comes to recognize, works through, tames and "disowns" her/his introjects, renders to the realm of other that which was felt to be self.

As these two findings regarding the redefinition of self and other are generalized to other relationships the client comes to reformulate notions of self and other on a broad front. This in turn opens the way to further redefinitions at higher levels of emotional development. Thus, the course of therapy can be conceived of as operating along the developmental lines described in Chapter V of this book. Thus, a clinician could use this scheme to organize their understanding of the client's developmental struggles. It is also important to bear in mind that clients are typically operating with a multiplicity of sub-personalities, each one working on its own developmental trajectory, sometimes mired in a conflictual morass.

The following examples will, I hope, show how cases may be usefully and interestingly formulated using these constructs.

B: Clincal Examples: Individuals

Dave came to counseling with the presenting problem of what he called "social phobia." He wanted to go to graduate school but was terrified when trying to enter the classroom. He had always felt like an outsider. He was the odd one out in his family. He was the intellectual. They liked popular television, football and Las Vegas. He had no chums as a boy and felt very alone. His social phobia could be understood as resulting from an overwhelming sense of alterity, of being radically different from the others. This difference, as is usual, was associated with feelings of fear, suspicion and paranoia. The transference relationship with Dave was very much like the "twinning" transference described by Kohut (1971, 1977). The feeling was very often one of "you are just like me." There was a similar and related feeling of egalitarian "chumship" between the therapist and Dave, very reminiscent of the "chumship" described by Sullivan (1953). Once the therapist had overcome his initial concerns about the countertransference and was able to both enjoy the sense of chumship while not forsaking an interpretive function, Dave moved forward. It was as if the experience of closeness and similarity with one another enabled him to cope with the radical "otherness" of the graduate school classroom.

Interestingly, Dave's forward progress was greatly assisted by a series of events that we saw as synchronicity, "signs," happy coincidences that gave him "lucky breaks" while also deepening in him a transcendent feeling of deep connectedness with others and the world.

Sally, too, presented with a serious social phobia, and this, too, was interfering with her forward progress. College classes were a torture to her, especially if they involved public speaking.

In counseling she told of a childhood of social ostracism and of being beaten by her angry sister. She was abandoned by her father and she felt that her resemblance to him led to her being excluded by the family at large who also treated her as if she was "odd" and "somehow very different." It was perhaps this chronic alienation that resulted in a deep feeling of "otherness" that she had. Much of the counseling had to do with helping her "read' social situations, to label feelings that she and others had and coming to accept them as ordinary, common, human experiences. An outgrowth of this seemed to be her feeling less "odd," more at home and more like others. It was as if a radical alterity that she felt was slowly overcome and replaced with a sense of familiarity and continuity. This was not a transcendent sense of fusion of self and other as described in the higher levels of Dabrowski's scheme (Chapter V) It was simply an everyday sense of being similar to and in contact with the other. As this feeling strengthened, her social phobia weakened and she was able to progress in school and career. I was reminded of a telling passage from the memoirs of U.S. Grant (1999). In it, he describes how, during the early days of his military expedition he was tracing and following the trail of his enemy down the Mississippi valley. He was filled with anxiety and trepidation until, with a flash of insight, he realized that his enemy was feeling just as much concern and anxiety, even dread, as was he. From this point on, his attitude changed, and he became more confident, even daring in his exploits.

While Dave and Sally felt estranged from others as a result of a chronic, cumulative trauma of being continually "othered" by their families, sometimes clients are radically othered by a short, sharp trauma. **Marnie**, for example, was traumatized upon discovering a cache of her father's violent pornography. "Who was this man?" she wondered. He was clearly other than she believed. A chasm, an unbridgeable rift formed between her as a young girl and her father, now a stranger. **Bronwyn** had a similar experience of traumatic alterity not only when sexually molested by her brother, but also when her mother refused to believe her when she told her of the abuse. In these instances, the individual is traumatically othered, isolated, estranged, cut off. This experience goes beyond the feeling of being alone, for this can be conceptualized by the individual. This radical alterity goes beyond thought; it is unthinkable, dreadful, stunning, and even awe-inspiring.

One of the clinical tasks, in addition to the many that have been addressed in the extensive literature on trauma and sexual molestation and abuse, is to help the client work through the experience of radical alterity and its sequalae. Simple acknowledgment of this experience of radical alterity in an empathic way can go a long way to overcoming the deep estrangement adhering to these dreadful experiences.

In other clinical situations the process is approximately reversed. That which was felt to be self is, as it were, extruded, and experienced as other. In clinical language, an introject is identified and then disowned and seen as not belonging to the self.

Luke, 45, was depressed and lonely. Although he longed to marry and have a family, he had never had a significant, long relationship with a woman and was despairing of ever doing so. In the course of therapy it emerged that in some ways he had introjected his controlling and possessive mother. It was as if he was a sort of *doppelganger*. Unawares, he was two people, himself and his mother. This couple, experienced as one, was unconsciously married and every time Luke started to have a successful relationship with a woman his jealous internalized "wife-mother," whom he experienced as a set of attitudes held by himself, would rear up in a jealous, possessive rage and cause him to end the relationship, usually by devaluing the woman. Luke would manifest these two subpersonalities in a striking way in therapy sessions. When speaking from "Luke" he would lean to one side of the seat. When speaking from "mother" he would lean to his right, the other side of the seat. In addition, when he was speaking as "defeated Luke," when his relationship had been successfully sabotaged by his internalized mother, he would slump forward, fold his feet under his calves and put his hands together in an upside-down prayer position, manifesting a hole between his thumbs and forefingers.

Gradually, by drawing his awareness to these three subpersonalities, Luke was able to effect a "divorce" from his internalized "wife-mother" (that he felt as himself) and live a life relatively free from "her" internalized sabotage. This was not always easy because, since "she" was an introject, Luke would experience her as a center of his own subjectivity. Ultimately that which was experienced as himself was to some extent expunged and seen as other.

José manifested a similar dynamic. At times, during sessions, he would suddenly change, perhaps spooked by a word or comment made by the counselor. He would shift from being warm, lively, humorous and engaging to being officious, hard-driving, angry, forceful and argumentative. As he engaged in these tirades, he was, as it were, caught up in them. Only after a year or so were we able to see that these "tirade states" were the result of him having introjected a sadistic, persecutory brother. As a young boy, he had shared a bedroom with his older brother who had chronically teased and tormented him. It was excruciatingly painful for José and he had coped by introjecting his brother and by repressing the elements of himself that had been linked to him. This introject, originating as "other" was now experienced (when it became partially conscious) as part of self. Through the course of therapy this introjected other was identified as such. It was rather like discovering one has a parasite, a sort of bodily "secret sharer," to introduce an alternative reading of Conrad's (1993) short story. As the strength of his introjects weakened and as it became perceived as more external to "self," more libidinal energy was released and José became more confident, got and kept a girlfriend and completed graduate studies.

A sudden alteration in the mental status of a close friend or loved one can precipitate a traumatic othering, a frightening sense of radical aloneness. **Janet** described how one morning when she was eleven years old, she was walking to school with a beloved friend who suddenly, out of the blue, stepped over to a pay phone, placed a call to the school they were headed to and called in a bomb threat. At that moment Janet described feeling as though the sidewalk just fell from underneath her feet. She realized that her friend had gone crazy. The feeling of easy familiarity, the sense of being at one with a near sister evaporated and was replaced with a sense of alien strangeness and distance. She felt bizarre.

A similar sensation was described by **Ken** as he described riding home on the subway after having witnessed a violent crime. He felt as though no one else could possibly know what he had just witnessed, and all the terrifying feelings and fantasies rushing through his mind. He felt cut off, alone.

Alterity: The Experience of the Other

Sometimes clients can present issues from a sense of alterity that involves deep connection with others, a kind of alterity involved in Jung's notion of the collective unconscious. **Freda** was a gifted journalist. However, she had a problem that she called "anxiety attacks." Frequently, while on assignment, she would suffer what she would call a "melt down" late at night in the hotel she was staying in while investigating what were often turbulent and painful conflicts in distant cities and towns. Although there had been some trauma in her childhood and adolescence, it was not particularly severe, although it could have been amplified by what Dabrowski would term high levels of overexcitability, especially emotional overexcitability. She was a gifted individual. She was also an extraverted, feeling, intuitive type, according to the Jungian typology. Based on this, she could be extremely open to the collective unconscious and she might be hit by waves of powerful images and affect from the collective unconscious of the communities she was investigating. I presented these ideas to her and they seemed plausible, especially since she sensed that these images and affects would, as it were, steal into her without her being aware of it. These incursions of powerful feelings and fantasies she would experience not as other but as herself and she would call them anxiety attacks. This theory seemed to "fit" for her; especially since she could see how such a proclivity would at the same time be both a blessing and curse, especially for a journalist. On the one hand she would be especially well-attuned to whatever was on the community's mind; on the other hand, she would be prey to extraordinarily powerful feelings and fantasies. The trick was to learn how to discriminate self from not self, to draw the boundaries between self and other more clearly. She went on to lead a very successful career as a writer.

Corinne came to counseling roughly on the one year anniversary of losing her fiancé in a terrible accident while on vacation. She was mourning and much of the counseling involved the working through of the trauma of losing a loved one suddenly and under violent circumstances. Corinne worked very hard at this painful process and was showing signs of being able to start life again, although slowly and reluctantly. As the treatment process was winding to a close, and Corinne was starting to talk of not needing counseling any more, she brought up one last thing that had always bothered her. It was as if she would need to settle this last issue if she was to be able to move on. She mentioned that both she and her fiancé had had premonitions of something terrible happening the very day before the accident and that they had resolved that they should leave as soon as possible. It was this premonition that had disturbed her. Jung, in his theory of the collective unconscious, admits of the possibility of deep connections between self and other and, through this, deep connections with the past and the future. We can thus see, in this example of a patient's premonition, a result of a special sense of alterity… a sense that needed sensitive empathic understanding. It is not at all uncommon in my practice for patients to have these "Jungian" types of experiences—remote viewing, premonitions, synchronicities, visitations. And it is important, I have found, for me to be flexible enough in my conceptions of alterity to follow the client where they need to go to fully realize the possibilities inherent in these special, unconventional forms of alterity.

Gerard, a forty-one year old aspiring novelist, provides us with an example of a dream that can be interpreted along alteric lines.

Alterity: The Experience of the Other

"I am in an atrium with vast curtain windows. Inside, it is hot and filled with exotic plants I have gathered from all over the world. It is rich and variegated, brimming with life. I go to the fogged window and anxiously, tentatively touch the glass..."

I offer the interpretation that this dream is about his writing and his anxiety about how it will be received by the world—by the others. He responds that this fits and then associates to the widely ranging ups and downs of his self esteem, especially as it concerns his writing. At times he believes he will be recognized as a member of the pantheon of the great writers and at other times he thinks he will amount to nothing. It is as if the "boy in the bubble," shut off from the outside world, is left in a state of narcissistic dysregulation and disorganization—paralyzed into inactivity by fantasies of grandiosity or nothingness.

I connect this to his relationship to his father who deserted him early in his life leaving him with two unintegrated paternal imagoes; one a God, one a nothing in an empty desert. I also surmise that his strong attraction to surrogate fathers—substitutes who exerted, in his words, "a siren call" over him and often lead him astray and harmed him, is related to his not having had a reliable father from whom he could separate and individuate in late adolescence (Blos,1985). This in turn links back to his uncertain isolation in the glassy atrium. Gerard's dream thus offers some fascinating insights into possible connections between alterity, creativity, separation, individuation, narcissism and father-son relationships.

Boris's story shows us how a traumatic loss in childhood can dramatically affect one's sense of alterity. Boris evidenced many features of an obsessive nature—tidiness, punctiliousness, high levels of anxiety, detail mindedness and deep concerns about failure and inadequacy. All of this combined with a goodly dose of somatization and hypochondriasis. He did however function well in college. He was in his middle twenties and had an active conventional social life. The focal trauma seemed to be the sudden death of his father while he was in the room when he was aged six. In addition to all the complications one might expect after such an experience, it was also important to explore the multiple forms of alterity he experienced in the wake of this terrible event. The trauma itself, an unexpected misfortune, made him painfully aware of the Otherness of the world, the Otherness of the Real, of his failing father's body, of death. In addition, after the event, he becomes identified as the child whose father died and this marks him as radically other, no less than the traumatic experience he has been through. He is cut off from others, painfully alienated. The empathic connectedness of the therapeutic relationship provided an important counterforce to these dynamics. Boris's story shows us that in addition to the complications of grieving and the shock that we encounter with persons who have been traumatized, we also must address the alterations in the sense of alterity. Sometimes this may require flexibility in the patient-therapist role. For example increased emotional availability of the therapist may be called for, along with an appropriate use of therapist transparency or sharing toward the end of increasing the sense of communion with others.

These clinical examples demonstrate, I trust, that new and potentially useful approaches to the therapeutic project are opened up through the application of the concept of alterity, especially if a broadened and deepened understanding of the many phases of this concept is employed. While some empirical work has been done in this area, there is still much to be done.

C: Clinical Examples: Alterity and Groups

"Signs in the street,
    that say where you're going,
Are somewhere
    Just being their own."

The Byrds, "Eight Miles High" (2006)

"I am me and you are he and he is me and we are all together"

John Lennon, "I am the Eggman" (2002)

The concept of alterity in the several forms outlined in this work can be found in the life of any group and the theory of alterity can provide a useful explanatory template for many group phenomena.

Groups in the "tavistock" tradition, laying bare, as they do in their pristine sparseness, covert processes in groups, provide many living examples of these assertions. Thus, many of the illustrations which follow will be drawn from these types of groups. An outline of the tavistock approach and tradition can be found in Bion (1961), Colman and Geller (1975) and Colman and Bexton (1985) and Hazell (2005a, b).

Perhaps the most radical experience of alterity occurs between the members of the group and the leader, therapist or consultant. The role difference is often experienced as a separating chasm, often widened with differences in authority, real of imagined. It is in the group that we witness very clearly the powerful ambivalences towards alterity. On the one hand the alterity is feared and hated and vigorous attempts must be made to capture and engulf the other so as to obliterate its radical separation. On the other hand, alterity is needed as a way of preserving an essential distance between self and other because the other is being used as a container for unwanted, split off and projected parts of the self. Furthermore, alterity is necessary in order to establish identity. Also, in the Levinasian sense, it is the other who beckons us on towards transcendence. However, while the alterity must be preserved, it must not, under the conditions of projective identification, be too radical or complete. The other, since it contains potentially dangerous entities that are also part of the self, must be only partially other. It must be shown to be under the control of the subject in significant ways.

Thus we will often see groups at first recoil in shock at the radical alterity of the leader. This initial shock is followed by a series of attempts that manifest this just-mentioned ambivalence. The group may try to "get a rise out of the leader" or may cause them to change their seat, break a smile. They may create a "simulacrum" of the leader or consultant – an ersatz leader who is one of them, not so radically other, yet not quite of them. They may exalt the leader so as to render them "other" and then de-skill them so as to render them "one of us." Leaders will thus feel pulled and pushed and manipulated rather like the spool of the "fort-da" game that Freud observes.

Alterity: The Experience of the Other

A parallel experience of radical alterity is often found at the boundary of a group when it makes contact with another group, as when, say, a visitor, perhaps a representative from another group, arrives. Sometimes a group will be stunned by the very evidence of the existence of another group because usually the boundaries are in no way prepared for such an encounter. It is as if the group has been operating under the aegis of a defense, the denial of alterity.

This encounter with the other, on a group level, usually stimulates much activity in the unprepared group. Much work is triggered as the group seeks to organize its boundary management, its gate keeping. A new set of roles has to evolve, and along with this a new authority system and a realignment of the tasks of the group to include interaction with the other groups. Questions must be addressed. Who will speak for us? Who are "we"? What will they say? How much time will we spend dealing with the other groups? How are we to understand them? What should our policy, our stance toward them, be? The experience of alterity stimulates complexity in the internal organization of groups.

The experience of alterity and the management of its anxiety-producing elements are always evident in intergroup relations. In one pattern, for example, the members of the group merge their individual identity with their group's identity, often accomplishing this by identifying with the leader. Another group is seen as the other, usually the inferior or "bad" other. As long as the other group is kept at a distance, it remains imaginary and anxiety in the group is low. If the other group is experienced as close at hand, or if a representative of the other group is encountered, anxiety, and perhaps dread, are felt and the group is liable to a paranoid response. This scenario is of course, the familiar "fight-flight" assumption described by Bion simply reframed in terms of the experience of alterity. Related dynamics can be frequently observed when two organizations merge or collaborate on a project.

Experiences in groups offer many opportunities to apply the conceptual scheme for understanding alterity outlined in Chapters IV and V. At times groups operate in a "fusional" way where selves and other are joined. Boundaries and individual differences can be obliterated as the group seems to "homogenize" itself into an amorphous lumpless puree. At other times, group can be seen to vigorously deny connection, to become atomized, hyper-individualized, as if no similarities or even contact points existed. The group in these states seems to operate under the assumption of radical alterity. And at yet other, less common, times the group seems to operate in a paradoxical state, profoundly connected, at one, and yet still soundly differentiated amongst its members.

These states can be arranged among the developmental continuum of Dabrowski's theory, as outlined in Chapter V of this book. The first and second states are to be found in the basic assumption groups described by Bion, as well as in conventionally arranged groups. The last example would correspond with Bion's "sophisticated" or "work" group or the "performing" stage of Tuckman's theory (cited in Pennington, 2002). Integrating these ideas with the theory of contemporaneous, unconscious imaginary groups (Hazell 2005), we arrive at the notion that every group, while it may manifest in its relatively conscious and easily observable proceedings, certain forms of alterity, it also contains, in its unconscious, group mentality, sets of imaginary groups adhering to different assumptions about the relatedness of self and other.

The fusional state of alterity is aptly described by LeBon (2002) and Freud (1975). Each offers somewhat different explanations for the "madness of crowds" but each is describing a group where individuality has melted into the mass, perhaps coalescing in the identification with an exalted leader. Similar states can be seen in what Janis (1989) describes as "groupthink." Here the group seems hell-bent on a given set of perceptions, cognitions, attitudes and beliefs and will not tolerate, indeed will punish, any differing opinion, any reminder that there is an other. These can be understood in part as a regressive moving towards an omnipotent frame of mind where all is inside the narcissistic orbit of the group. Nothing must surprise, everything is already explained. These regressions will occur where there is too much helplessness, where there is trauma or such a high rate of change that other more reality-oriented coping mechanisms are overwhelmed and abandoned.

Groups in this state are quite prone to paranoid ideation, fantasies and structures. Inevitably, something other-than-us does show up and fight-flight tendencies as described by Bion (1961), emerge. For example, at the beginning of "Tavistock" conferences, it is customary for the staff to walk in, together and on time, and take their pre-arranged seats in front of the members. The staff, in its role boundedness, timeliness, organization and different professional clothing is experienced by the members as very *"other-than-us"* and usually stimulates anxious paranoid fantasies, for example, of the SS or of prison wardens. Similarly, at the beginning of small study groups, the entrance of the consultant, with their clear alterity, evokes frightening and disruptive persecutory anxieties, often followed by attempts at "capture." The group will attempt to reduce or obliterate the otherness of the consultant, perhaps by getting them to break role and behave like a member, perhaps by ignoring them, perhaps by shutting them out.

In these observations we notice interesting connections between taking up a role, formal and informal, the establishment of an alterity and the stimulations of persecutory anxiety. Perhaps this is a universal anxiety in the establishment of functioning social systems, since all these depend on roles and role boundaries. To state this in reverse: Organization entails roles, roles entail boundaries, boundaries imply alterity, alterity is met with anxiety—a complex anxiety, often persecutory, sometimes hopeful, sometimes terrifying, awesome, sometimes relieving. This relief, is often, however, only temporary, for the relief achieved by using the other as a repository of unwanted self-part-objects (and its associated death instinct) is quickly followed upon by a persecutory dread of their vengeful return.

In these descriptions of the other, it is my contention that the other of the staff, the consultant, the other group is experienced in the register of Lacan's *l'objet grand A* (other with a big "O"). This is the Other that is truly Other, almost the Other one dare not name or "mess with." In reaction to this, one may often see (both in individuals and in groups) attempts to manufacture, create and sustain *l'objet petit a* (the other with a little "o") of Lacan. This I regard as the object suffused with and elaborated by very strong imaginational elaborations. These elaborations help, as it were, "soften the blow" of the other, rendering fuzzy the boundaries between self and other and filling in the gaps between self and other.

This, I believe can be regarded as the same domain as the transitional object of D.W. Winnicott (1965a). The transitional object is an object one may "monkey around with," play with (assimilate, in the Piagetian sense of the word). At one moment the transitional object is other, it has a life of its own; at the next it is one with the child. In this fluidity, flexibility and saturation with imaginational elaborations, the transitional object is *l'objet petit a*.

Groups will create transitional phenomena, sometimes rather akin to mascots or in the form of group fantasies, myths and religions. There, transitional phenomena serve the same function for the group. For example, in a group I was consulting to one female member brought a small stuffed animal to groups. She named the animal "Bumpy" and Bumpy became a central person in the life of the group. Most people liked him but some members resented him and what he stood for. For some he represented comfort and intimacy, while for others he stood for a claustrophobic and stifling closeness. The group both came together and remained apart around Bumpy. These phenomena could be interpreted many ways. For example, perhaps Bumpy stood for the consultant after having been operated upon by wish fulfillment. The radical alterity of the consultant was transformed through Bumpy from *l'autre grand A* to *l'autre petit a.*

Frequently individuals and sub groups find themselves structurally, perhaps spatially, located between two parties that are struggling with issues of alterity. This in- between group can often serve as a transitional area for these two parties. For example, I have for many years consulted to groups of graduate students involved in an experiential here and now learning group in the "tavistock" tradition. (Colman and Geller, 1975). In this work I always have two student co-leaders who also consult to the group. It is routine for these two co-leaders, who occupy an intermediary role as students and consultants between myself (faculty) and the group (students), to be subjected to considerable pressures. They are the ones who are called, questioned, challenged, cornered, and interrupted. The faculty member is left alone. It is as if the student co-leaders are a relatively unprotected nation lying between two powerful nations – the well-known "buffer state." The angle of interpretation here, however, is from the vantage point of alterity. Where an institutional design creates roles that accentuate or lay bare an alterity and there is a buffer zone or buffer roles, much of the anxiety stimulated by this alterity will be played out (unconsciously dramatized) in this transitional zone. This awareness can help organizations, leaders and members insofar as when one is aware of this dynamic one can, to some extent, be prepared for some of the pressures and perhaps inoculate oneself from some of the negative consequences. This awareness can also be helpful insofar as social systems, in order to buffer distressing alterities, will often create departments or roles whose covert function it is to quell or defend against them. It can be helpful to know to what extent this is part of one's covert job description or departmental mission.

At times negotiations between parties, organizations and groups break down. During these times of very high tension the sense of otherness can be extremely high, so high that the sense of alterity becomes what can be termed <u>radical alterity</u>. The experience of radical alterity can be understood as the condition where the other is experienced not as different only in degree, but also as a difference in kind; and not of a difference in kind that can be calibrated with concepts and dimensions already in one's possession. In radical alterity, the other exists outside of one's "cognitive map," their otherness is beyond the pale, unthinkable. This very unthinkability of the other is anxiety-producing. In addition, this unthinkability leads to extreme difficulties in cognition, in conceptualization. Bion's theory of thinking leads us to conclude that this increases dramatically the likelihood of what he would call "A6" activity, to refer to Bion's grid (1977), activity which can perhaps be called "acting out." We now arrive at the point where unreflected-upon-action is highly likely. This action is also going to contain elements that stand for the radical alterity. These acts will be unthinkable, beyond the pale, beyond bizarre, beyond belief. Terrorism, sabotage, torture, mutilation, crimes against humanity, genocide; many of these can be interpreted along these lines. Viewed from this perspective, one could make an argument that individuals and institutions would benefit from insights, procedures and structures that help manage, contain and yoke these powerful forces, deriving from disruptive experiences of alterity. Some organizations employ diversity specialists or have diversity awareness programs. These are excellent ideas, but perhaps only a beginning insofar as many of these cope with more available forms of alterity, not the radical alterity under discussion here.

It could be argued that the quest for knowledge has, at its root, a paranoid motivation. Something is seen to exist beyond us, this something affects us, could harm us and we are driven to master it, to understand it, to control it lest it control us. This seems to me to be linked to Klein's "epistemophilic instinct," the desire to know, to understand and explain. Klein links this with a quest to find and know the contents of our mother's body, including the unborn babies. In addition, since the other contains in phantasy unwanted, projectively identified parts of the self, there is involved in a desire to know the other, a deeper wish to know and master the self.

Levinas, in "Alterity and Transcendence," seems to posit that there are certain forms of alterity that are so extreme that we should simply accept them; that any attempt to bridge the chasm will be futile. It is better in these instances for the parties, be they individuals or groups, to simply accept this radical alterity. Neither party oppresses the other nor interferes with them, yet the difference is not ignored or swept away in clichés or denial. Given the human tendency to fear the other and to utilize projective identification, these relationships are very fragile and all too easily slip into conflict.

The dynamics of alterity are frequently observable in families. The tension one can see in families during wedding ceremonies can be understood as emanating in part from the encounter of two family groups each experiencing the other family as "other," yet as an "other" group that is soon to be part of one's own group. The other group can be experienced in all the complex ways mentioned so far as a feuding partner, as new, exciting, hopeful, bizarre, exotic, self-enhancing or degrading. Typically these anxieties are bound in and channeled by rituals.

Blended families, families with stepchildren, foster children and stepparents all must cope with issues related to alterity. The family in these instances is not homogeneous in its members. Some individual or subgroup comes from "somewhere else," another family. Recently, with increasing frequency, someone in the family might be visibly "other" insofar as they are assigned to a different race. In my book "Family Systems Activity Book" (2006) I describe how the "odd person out" can more easily become the target of projective identification and thus serve as a repository or scapegoat for unconscious processes in the family, or any group for that matter.

In addition, as pointed out by Bowen (1994) and Guerin (1976) the other can serve as a safety net, as a third point outside of a pairwise relationship to help protect members of the pair from anxieties having to do with engulfment and abandonment. Examples of this abound; a classic is where a couple "recruits" a third party for an affair and this third party helps members of the pair to be comfortably uncomfortable about being abandoned or engulfed. In these cases the other is held on to and yet not fully accepted, and is ambivalently used until the couple resolves their issues around abandonment and engulfment, if they ever do. This other need not always be a person; they could be a hobby, a mission, an addiction or a cause.

Not only do individuals encounter and cope with alterity, groups of all sizes must deal with the panoply of feelings and fantasies stimulated by the varying perceptions of the other. Lawrence (2007) in his work on "social dreaming" implies an alterity that is significantly different from the conventional one. As a technique, it involves a group of individuals assembling, sharing their dreams, and reflecting, in a systematic fashion, upon the ways in which these dreams uncover and relate to unconscious aspects of social realities.

> *"When three or more persons are together, the chances are that their unconscious minds will resonate; the unconscious images will resonate …because the unconscious web of emotions is unconstrained by the demands of relationship."(Lawrence, 2007, p.15)*

This quasi merging of the individual into the group unconscious occurs because, "in dreaming we are less "egocentric" for the "I" is less important as we lose ourselves in the dream." (Lawrence 2007, p.7)

These ideas lead us to a distinct and interesting sense of alterity. In a fashion similar to that conceived by Jung, we are connected to the other through a form of collective unconscious. However, we do not find archetypes as we do with Jung. The code for reading the dream is not as driven by these innate collective thought structures. It is more indeterminate and flexible. Lawrence's ideas are also connected to work in the tavistock tradition (Coleman and Geller, 1975). In this work, conventional notions of self and other are often suspended or disrupted by notions of a group mentality in which members participate by making contributions and withdrawals of parts of themselves. Conventional senses of self and other are thus undermined by assumptions that individuals can contain split off, projected and introjected parts of others. This theme is concisely depicted by Wells (in Colman and Geller, 1985).

Church *et al* (2009) describe a technique wherein art projects created in or by a group can be used as a means for reading the group unconscious. This technique, in a manner similar to Lawrence's social dreaming, implies an unconventional notion of alterity.

D. Trauma, Groups and Alterity

We can attempt to understand the social group from a number of perspectives. Each of these perspectives rests in part on different assumptions regarding alterity, or the nature of the boundaries that exists between the individuals comprising the group.

In group-as-a-whole work ("Tavistock" groups) there is an assumption that, at an unconscious level, individuals in groups are often intimately connected, perhaps even at times fused, with one another.

Thus, in this type of work with groups the appearance of the separateness of individuals in a group is regarded as only the tip of the iceberg. In the unconscious, one finds different alterities. Identities fuse, merge and separate. Members of the group may lose themselves in the group or in others, or may separate and isolate themselves. Metaphorically, the group may be like a bag of billiard balls, hard and differentiated in a state of what might be called radical self protective alterity, or the group may be likened to a mass of melted candles, where all the wax has liquefied and fused into an undifferentiated mass.

Hopper (2003) argues that, when a group must deal with trauma in some way, so it will tend to shift into one or the other, or both of these alteric states. Trauma may be visited upon a group in multiple ways. Thus there are multiple ways in which the group may become profoundly undifferentiated or radically self protectively alteric. Hopper points out that these oscillations are parallel to the adaptations Tustin (1972, 1990) observes in autism.

Sometimes a group is traumatized by external events—economic setbacks, death, disaster, plague, persecution, war and so on. Groups can also be traumatized insofar as they contain a member or some members who have been traumatized and who have not fully worked through this trauma. The relatively unworked trauma thus becomes part of the group's unconscious. Trauma can also be visited upon a group through intergenerational transmission. For example, several members of a group may be grandchildren or great grandchildren of people who were traumatized by one or several of the litany of traumatic events both personal and historical in scale—war , slavery, class oppression, genocide, sexual assault, murder.

In my experience, if even one person is carrying unworked trauma, powerful, incompletely metabolized and unworked, they can exert an extraordinarily powerful impact on the experiences of alterity in the group, resulting in dynamics very similar to those described by Hopper (i.e. massification or aggregation). For example, in one group I observed one member dominate the sessions with lectures on sexism, silencing the males with moralizing tirades and exhorting the women to be ever more vigilant and angry about their oppression. Any attempts to interpret events along any lines other than gender were regarded as a betrayal of the true cause. The group clammed up in fear of being singled out as being sexist or an improper person. Of course sexism is oppressive and bad and should be reversed in the spirit of freedom and personal development, but in this group one was reminded of Orwell's *Animal Farm* (2004) where the pigs take over, at first with good intentions, but only later to become oppressive and paranoid. It was as if there existed, in the group, an invisible and frightening secret police that squelched spontaneity and signs of free life.

At root, this could be understood as a phobic and distressed response to alterity, stemming from trauma that had not been worked through. Taussig (1992) accurately, I believe, asserts that all unexpected misfortune is alteric. That is to say, all trauma painfully reminds us of self-other boundaries. Trauma has the effect of creating a sense of our own otherness – the more intense the trauma, the more radical is the alterity. Thus, we can expect in groups that include in their membership individuals who have experienced trauma (or who contain trauma owing to transgenerational transmission of trauma) methods of coping with alterity that are different from those found in groups that do not contain traumatized members.

Hopper (2003) and Ganzerain (1989) are among several writers who have written on this topic. Hopper argues that in groups that contain trauma there is often an oscillation between the "basic assumptions" (Bion 1961), that is, unconscious attitudes, of aggregation and massification. These two conditions, which Hopper explicitly derives from Tustin's ideas on the development of autism, are reactions in the domain of self-other boundaries to trauma (Tustin, 1972, 1990).

In the instance of aggregation, the individual adopts a hard shell, a "crustacean" form of adaptation. A group operating under the aegis of the basic assumption of aggregation might be metaphorized as a bucket of crabs or a sack of billiard balls – hard cases all, with no melting into one another. Hopper further points out that this basic assumption will often be "personified." An individual will frequently become an aggregation leader. This individual acts as a spokesperson for hyper-alterity, for super-individualism, and oftentimes becomes a central person in the group, pursuing these ends frequently through exerting interpersonal pressure, sometimes with an ideology, yet unconsciously they are motivated by a panicked response to the increased alterity of traumatic experience.

This basic assumption of aggregation will, in Hopper's opinion, oscillate back and forth from its opposite partner, the basic assumption of massification. In this it is as if the members become amoeboid and merge with one another in a fused, undifferentiated mass. The shock of the other that is experienced in trauma is responded to in this instance by the other being psychologically obliterated and merged into one undifferentiated glob. Again, groups will often personify this process and elect a massification leader, an individual who, owing to their special preparation, or their structural position, takes up the role of creating, sustaining, leading and at times enforcing a massified group.

A group operating under the aegis of aggregation might have the motto of, "I do my thing, you do yours," coupled with a disdain for signs that one is affected by, or has an effect on, or others. A massification group, on the other hand, will have intense anxiety and difficulty in dealing with differences between people. Groups will often oscillate confusingly between these two assumptions and since anxiety is high, both forms of the group will often be "policed" by those who are ready willing and able to take up this controlling function in the group.

Given that trauma is so widespread, that there is considerable evidence pointing toward the intergenerational transmission of trauma and that the impacts of secondary and even tertiary trauma have been shown to be significant and long lasting, given that humans must operate in groups in order to accomplish their ends, it would seem that this line of thinking opened up by Hopper and addressed here is indeed worthy of further exploration.

Chapter III: Alterity All Around

"A direct consequence of the alienation of man from the product of his labor, from his life activity and his species life is that man is alienated from other men. When man confronts himself he also confronts other men. What is true of man's relationship to his work, to the product of his work and to himself, is also true of his relationship to other men, to their labor and to the objects of their labor."

Karl Marx (1844/1961, p103)

A: A Potpourri of Experiences of Alterity

This series of vignettes attempts to capture aspects of the experience of alterity. They demonstrate that the experience of otherness is one that suffuses everyday life, and that often occurs in the context of other thoughts and feelings.

The first vignette captures some of the sense of shock and strangeness when another person unexpectedly interprets an event differently from us, jerking us out of an habitual expectation that others will see the world as we do.

!Nai and the student

I was teaching a class called "Social Issues and Technology." As a means of showing how a socio-technical system such as hunting and gathering could be destroyed by being overrun by an industrial society, and to demonstrate the negative, complex and painful effects of "reservationization" of a previously mobile people, I showed the documentary "!Nai, The Story of a !Kung Woman." (1980, Marshall, Meismer). I showed the movie to the crowded class of about forty students, had the students discuss some questions on the movie in small groups and hand in their responses.

The next day, I return to my office and find a vituperative message on my telephone from one of the students accusing me of racism. I had, she claimed, in showing this movie, insulted black people by presenting them in a negative light, dispossessed and riddled with conflict. She complained to my boss, the dean, and threatened legal action. Any attempt at dialogue was thwarted, so deep was her fury.

I felt terrible, like the bottom of my stomach had fallen out. I felt very alone and deeply misunderstood. I had made such efforts to present the video in a balanced way and to demonstrate the destructive cruelty unleashed against the !Kung. But the difference was intractable. The sense of the "otherness" of this student was radical.

Even when it later turned out that the student had missed the first part of the class and had only seen the last 30 minutes or so of the film, no rapprochement was possible. This person's "take" on the reality of the situation was completely at odds with mine. Who was she? Where was she coming from? There was no common ground. The otherness, if not absolute, was radical.

Eventually, the problem went away. I made a short speech to the class (who did not share this student's view of the import and meaning of the video), and made alterations to the class, including more material and a video on minority inventors. I developed a new unit for the class, entitled, "Who Invents?" and encouraged students to think critically on the topics of class, race, ethnicity and invention. I made changes in my practice but still, the extreme otherness of this student's reaction stays with me rather like an undissolved particle or an undigested lump in my memory. This experience points to the possibility that such radical alterity can lead to creativity and social development.

This next vignette captures the sense of otherness that can occur when an experience, in and of itself, is hard to digest or assimilate. It forces recognition of the separateness of our wills from events in the world.

Ben and a sequence of bad experiences

A client, Ben, comes to a session stating that he needs to process a slew of recent events. A friend of his, a psychotherapist, had a client die suddenly and violently. Another friend discovers her husband is HIV positive. The sister of his ex-wife drowns. He himself develops symptoms that make him concerned for his health. He finds that, try as he might, he cannot "wrap his arms around" these experiences. However, he does believe there are lessons to be learned from them, but still elements remain beyond the pale, inassimilable into his world view. I suggest that perhaps the very fact that there are these inassimilable elements of experience is part of the lesson.

I note to myself that this is in line with Lacan's notion of the Symbolic, Imaginary and the Real. Some aspects of life cannot be encoded in either the Symbolic or Imaginary realm. They remain in the domain of the "Real," in the domain of the radically other.

Interestingly, Ben interspersed his presentation with a joke or two, significant among these was the following from Rodney Dangerfield:

> *"I don't know, what a day! I go to open the door, and it falls off. I go to open the window and the handle breaks off. You know, I'm scared to go to the bathroom!"*

Embedded in the evocative themes of shock, breaking and loss is the anxiety of loss of the phallus, of castration anxiety.

I note to myself that it is not only the symbolic realm, with its rules of language that limits and "castrates"; it is the radical alterity of the Real in its inassimilability that foreshortens and emasculates our phallic potentialities.

This next example is similar to the first one, except that it addresses unacknowledged alterity in a colonial situation where an attempt at religious conversion is being essayed.

!Nai and the Preacher

In the movie "!Nai, The Story of a !Kung Woman," (1980) there is a very telling scene where a Christian minister is preaching to a group of !Kung about Jesus in his encounter with the woman at the well. Interviewed later, the preacher claims he was inculcating the virtues of spirituality and fidelity. !Nai, however, has a radically different take on the parable. "What was that woman thinking going to the well with that strange man? That Jesus must have been a bad man!" she exclaims.

The difference on "takes" of the parable is radical. There is no discernible overlap in their meanings. They do not complement one another, nor can they easily coexist as parallel interpretations, enriching one another.

Significant, too, is the lack of discourse between !Nai and the preacher. He is sure his point has been made. She is confused as to why such a tale of questionable behavior should be held up as an example. The preacher is operating on the assumption of some self-other continuity or contiguity, unaware that the alterity or separation is radical.

Sometimes the experience of alterity arrives when we find out that we really do not know someone like we thought we did. We can feel very close to someone, only to find out something secret and be jarred into a realization that they are very different, very separate, very "other." This following vignette illustrates this.

The discovery of an affair

Jake had been with Melanie for two years. They had fallen in love at first sight and were passionately in love. They joked at how they spent long languorous hours "gazing into each other's eyes in jasmine-scented rooms," locked in a symbiotic embrace.

However, while they felt at one with each other, they also had vicious fights when they would become possessive, suspicious and jealous. Jake, however, always felt secure in the relationship until one day, running through the park he happened upon Melanie in the arms of another man.

A flood of feelings surged through him: rage, betrayal, raw pain, sadness, jealousy. Among these was the feeling that he no longer "knew" Melanie. The sense of being at one with her was gone. She was "othered" by this experience. Clearly she was a center of initiative separate from him, capable of having secrets, capable of being separate. Perhaps this sense of alterity was the most shocking part of the whole experience.

Giving Instructions

In this everyday event of giving instructions to another we can observe some of the dynamics of alterity.

"It's in the refrigerator, on the left."

"Where? I can't see it."

"You can't see it! It's right there, right in front of you!"

It is as if the one making the request cannot believe that the other cannot see what they "know" to be there. I argue that a vital component of the frustration of this situation is its evidencing of alterity, of the separateness of the other. To some, this realization is manageable; to others, it is traumatic.

A hair in one's food

You are enjoying some food, you are hungry and it tastes good, looks good. Suddenly you see it, a hair on your plate. It is as if the spell is broken. A wave of disgust, almost nausea passes over you. You might think, "Well, it is a *cooked* hair. All the germs have been killed," but it makes no difference. The hair could be sterile, but the sense of disgust remains. Why? Perhaps because the hair is evidence of alterity, the witness to the otherness of that which one was to eat. Prior to the discovery of the hair, the food is experienced as almost self—soon it will be ingested and will become part of one's tissue. The waste will be excreted and become other in the form of urine and feces.

But the fantasy, while eating, is that the food about to be placed in one's mouth is self or almost self. The hair is a stark proof of its radical alterity. The food then quickly and decisively migrates to the region of *that which is radically other*. Typical contents of this region or category are feces, urine, strangers, the bizarre, shameful, forbidden, taboo and disgusting. The food is no longer, in good conscience, edible. The notion of alterity provides us with a different "take" on orality and anality, a take close to that described in Erikson's "Childhood and Society" (1963).

The examples proliferate, until you have alterity on the brain. In every moment there exists the possibility of an experience that will convince us of our profound oneness with others and, at the same time of the radical alterity of the other. While awareness of these shifts in the experience of alterity can help organize many phenomena, it is also small wonder that so frequently we slide into the everyday, conventional sense of self and other.

B: The Social Management of Alterity

The "other" presents us with the future and possibilities and a chance for growth. The other also presents us with the possibility of annihilation. We thus both wish to encounter and to avoid encountering the other. Out of this conflict develop what can be regarded as compromises (perhaps neurotic) between these two imperatives. These compromises only provide the semblance of alterity. They thus avoid the experience of risk involved in encountering the other. Unfortunately, also missing is the possibility of the beyond, of the future. The result is a sense of safety (at least in the short term) but also stasis, or stagnation.

Many sociocultural phenomena exemplify this condition. A prominent example is the shopping mall. Much has been written on malls (*The Malling of America, Kowinski, 1985*) and their social significance. *The Arcades Project* by Walter Benjamin (2002) documents and reflects upon the arcade, an early form of shopping mall in late 19th century Paris.

The mall invites us in with a promise of diversity, of difference, of encounters with the new, and yet it is a carefully managed diversity and novelty. It simulates an open-air marketplace and yet its boundaries are only semi-permeable such that the likelihood of encountering the radically other is minimized inside this comfortable bubble. The mall is not a deeply transformative environment. It is padded and softened to provide the experience of pseudo-alterity, pseudo-differences, and to enable and encourage the narcissism of small differences.

Similar to this is the phenomenon of the vacation resort. We are picked up at the airport by a brightly uniformed attendant and smoothly driven, in air-conditioned comfort, to the hotel. The hotel is similar in its basic structure and procedures to other chains of hotels, yet enough in the way of décor is different to provide the experience of novelty. But not too much novelty. The hotel is inside a gated community. (This walling off is sometimes obvious and explicit, sometimes subtle and surreptitious.) Nonetheless, the life of the surrounding region is only allowed in a very controlled, homogenized fashion. Beach vendors must have permits. The life of the street, village and marketplace is a cab ride away. All in all the experience is akin to a well-managed, expensive sanitarium, but a sanitarium with no invasive or disruptive therapeutics. Even the food has "alien" content removed. "Spiciness" is an imitation of spiciness. The music and entertainment is homogenized so as to not offend, intimidate or provoke. Thus, one can travel to "Bali," "Mexico," or "Jamaica" without ever actually encountering anything "other."

The phenomenon of the "brand image" seems to operate in a similar manner. Many products are produced by oligopolistic corporations. A few companies manufacture the bulk of certain goods or services. These goods and services become quite similar in many ways (for example, many beers, cigarettes, gasoline, automobiles) and the firms spend large sums to create the image of difference such that the experience of changing brands is portrayed as shifting from "one" to the "other." In the process, the consumer has become different, "other" than he or she was. In this way we witness the "manufacture of alterity," or more realistically, the manufacture of a pseudo-alterity.

Levinas argues that the other poses, for us, the possibility of renewal, of transcendence. As such, the other is to be honored and valued. As such, the other stands for a deep human yearning for self-transcendence. It is as if the advertising industry knows how to tap into this deep longing for the experience of alterity while at the same time catering to the human anxiety of confronting the "Other." The result is the brand, the shopping experience, "exoticism," the ersatz adventure that provides a simulacrum of alterity—alterity without any threat of annihilation or self-dispersal, but also without any chance of self transcendence. The result—stagnant despair.

Much of this results from the oligopolization of production, namely, from the fact that many goods and services (gasoline, beer, food, communications, automobiles, clothing, banking) are provided by a small group of providers who engage in very muted and careful competition. Consumers, however, feel a need for recognition, for being seen as unique. Companies respond to this by providing brands that give the appearance of difference. Individuals, encouraged by advertising, come to base their identities on the "unique" and different products they consume. Thus emerges the phenomenon of the "narcissism of small differences." One can achieve a superficial sense of one's uniqueness, an ersatz sense of otherness that is only a mask for an underlying uniformity and sameness. One metaphorically enters a mall, populated with boutiques, each offering an opportunity to express, through one's choices of consumption, one's unique identity. The boutiques, however, are mostly owned by a self-regulating small group of co-operating companies. One's sense of individuality and, by extension, the sense of otherness gained this way is a fantasy.

In some respects, this ersatz otherness represents an example of Marcuse's notion of "repressive desublimation," (1964) where a transformative radical urge is met by the powers that be and re-molded into a simulacrum of transformation—a simulacrum, that, far from engendering a transformation of the status quo, actually supports and nourishes it. Thus, in this case, the quest for the recognition of uniqueness (the transformative radical urge) is yoked into the increased materialistic consumption of goods and services to accentuate narcissistic small differences.

It is this capacity of the pre-existing system (of economy, politics, psychology and values) to absorb the other and use it to its own ends that is addressed in Buñuel's *The Discreet Charm of the Bourgeoisie*, (1972) where a witty urbane group of middle class people sit down to enjoy dinner. Outrageous events occur, at first invading the smooth flow of their dinner conversation, but after a short while, they adapt and go on as before. Time after time, interruption after interruption, almost without losing a beat, they continue smoothly along.

The experience of alterity, in its raw form, is not an easy one. When we confront otherness we experience an array of emotions: awe, wonder, fear, confusion, doubt, shame. For while the other represents the future, novelty and hope, it also represents that over which we have no control, the other beyond our omnipotent orbit of control, beyond words. It can be an affront to our narcissism, and we may feel threatened with feelings of shame or fragmentation. The experience of radical alterity can also remain just that; the other can remain radically Other, beyond our reach, beyond dialogue, as Levinas so ably describes. Given this, it is not surprising that people, while yearning for the experience of the other, also fear it and are willing on many occasions to use an opportunity to reduce the experience of alterity and satisfy themselves with an experience of pseudo alterity.

Alterity: The Experience of the Other

Examples of these kinds of "compromise formations" between the wish to have and the wish to avoid, the experience of alterity can be found not only in consumer activity, vacation resorts, theme parks and individual behavior, but also in organizational behavior.

Many organizations have "diversity programs" aimed at increasing employee awareness of differences having to do with gender, age and ethnicity. While these programs have the laudable goals of fairness and equal opportunity and much yet remains to be done to uphold human rights in organizations of all kinds, especially on a global scale, these programs in managing diversity may not ultimately address the deeper issues of radical alterity.

For the experience of radical alterity is a desired but troublesome one. In confronting diversity, managers may opt to avoid the troublesome and anxiety-producing aspects of the experience of alterity and settle for a program that resembles more of a "shopping mall" approach to diversity. Participants select ethnicities and genders, ages and identities from an array of boutiques, often very well provisioned but lacking the Levinasian transcendence of the Other that stuns us and beckons us forward.

C: Sex and Alterity

The sexual encounter presents possibilities for the full array of the experiences of self and other. Sex is central in people's reaction to and expression of fundamental experiences of self and other. That this is so is to some degree evidenced in the slang references we find to sexual intercourse. In England it is sometimes referred to as, "a bit of the other," while in the U.S.A. it is sometimes called, "a piece of strange."

Embedded in these slang terms we find all the multilayered meanings and ambivalence typical of slang and human reactions to alterity. On the one hand sex is exciting because it offers an opportunity of encountering the other, that which is beyond. Involved in this is also the thrill and potential danger of the 'strange' in the other, the "stranger danger." Also embedded in these slang terms are the alternate experiences of oneself in sexual encounters. One is taken beyond oneself; one becomes other.

Willi Hoffer (1951) and Mahler (1975) both argue that it is through the sense of touch that we first encounter ideas of self-other differentiation. When we touch ourselves on the face we receive two signals, one from our hand and one from our face. When we touch someone else's face or when we are touched on the face, we receive only one signal, that emanating from either the face or the hand. These discriminations provide the bedrock of self-other differentiation. As argued elsewhere, for a variety of reasons, individuals will have a wide array of complex reactions to these early experiences of self and other. These reactions will manifest themselves in individual's preferred sexual behaviors and

Alterity: The Experience of the Other

fantasies. For example, some individuals may be traumatized by these early awarenesses of self-other differentiation. They maybe became aware too soon of the other and the ensuing sense of separation frightened them so much that they recoiled into a preferred quasi-autistic fantasy where either "there is no other" or "if there is an other, it is so much under my control that it is like an extension of me." This translates into a sexuality that is highly controlled, depersonalized, distant, ritualized, unrelated and essentially masturbatory. A spontaneous movement from the other, or an unexpected touch, is felt as a trauma, a trauma of otherness which recapitulates the earlier traumatic awareness of alterity. Compulsive masturbation, repetitive obsessive use of pornography, "tele sex" or sexual abstinence frequently fit in to this category. I say frequently, not always, for the same behavior can be accompanied by a wide array of fantasies which bespeak different relations of self and other. Furthermore, individuals will also oscillate, in response to life stressors, amongst different alterities. An individual with a "transcendent" notion of alterity might, under certain stresses, regress (perhaps temporarily) to the more autistic – like position considered here. Perhaps this regression might be a *reculer pour mieux sauter*, a regression in the service of the ego.

Conversely, there are individuals to whom this type of depersonalized sexuality is virtually unthinkable. They may try to masturbate but find it unexciting and meaningless, not because they are inhibited or guilty, but because it is as if they are locked into a sexuality that has to be with an other. Sexuality for them has to involve themselves with an other or Other, and that other must be clearly in evidence.

As we move toward the middle range of the alterity continuum (Chapter V) so we encounter the many common sexual phenomena of everyday life. For example, part of what Reich (1942) calls erosion of sexual excitement that occurs with couples who have been together a long while, can be understood as resulting from an incremental erosion of the exciting, perhaps anxiety producing, sense of alterity that the couple felt in the earlier days of their relationship. As time passes by, familiarity with each other increases, habits entrench and the sense of the partner being "other" diminishes as the (often comforting) sense of continuity with the other, the idea that they contain no new surprises, increases. Sometimes this process, perhaps combined with the other dissatisfactions and conflicts (conflicts involving separation and individuation, fears of engulfment or abandonment), leads to one partner or the other having sexual relationships outside the marriage. It is a challenge for couples in longer lasting relationships to do the personal work and the self-challenging necessary such that there is a continued sense of otherness, of the newness and difference of the other. Often, couples presume this involves an exploration of exoticism in their sexual life; new fantasies, new costumes, new places, new scenarios. Perhaps ignored, however, are deeper and more challenging possibilities of personality or behavior change in other realms, in which one partner goes through a "sea change," becomes a different person. Of course, these changes can be difficult and disruptive, but they can also provide for an exciting renewal of the sense of alterity. For many, however, the characterological rigidity is so great, and societal options so few that sexual dulling, with its negative *sequelae*, sets in.

These ideas are echoed in the research on child betrothal (reported in Heider, 2006). In these cases children are betrothed at an early age and live with one another almost as brother and sister prior to puberty. Apparently in these cases where familiarity is arguably high and the

Alterity: The Experience of the Other

sense of alterity is low the level of sexual attraction in the relationship is low, lower than in cases where couples do not live together in such close contact prior to marriage.

At the other extreme of this continuum are taboos regarding marriage or sexual pairing with individuals who are too much "the other," people from too far away, from a different clan, tribe or religious group. Here, we find taboos that prohibit marriage inside one's clan or village. One's betrothed must be other, but not too Other. Where the line is drawn varies with a host of cultural variables.

We can also find examples of sexuality as it might be at the "transcendent" end of the alterity continuum. This would also involve Levinas' thinking on "the caress." In this type of sexuality, one's sexual partner is experienced paradoxically as self and other, as an indiscriminable part of oneself <u>and</u> as a radically separate other. One melts into the other, becomes part of them and is simultaneously isolated from this ineffable, incommunicable other. In this form of sexuality one both participates in the totality and is taken to the edge of oneself. Much of Levinas' writing seems to have this tone, and in his (controversial) statements asserting that the other, being feminine, takes us beyond ourselves, I find a distinct erotic overtone.

Some religions explicitly make this link of certain forms of sexual excitement and the sense of alterity. Hindu temples exist that radically place eroticism at the center of means of achieving transcendent, beyond-the-self experiences. Sufi mystical poetry often has this transcendent erotic tone.

Similarly some psychologists have taken this bold step, notably Wilhelm Reich and Alexander Lowen. Such efforts however, are counter to many forces in current culture and while vigorous associations have formed around the thinking of both these men, their ideas have had some difficulty gaining acceptance in the "mainstream" psychologies, most of which, as I have argued previously, are based upon other, more limited, assumptions regarding alterity.

We can see here how the categories of different forms of alterity serve as an organizer for a wide array of sexual encounters and this organizer relates potentially to other systems in a fashion that is possibly predictive and explanatory.

Chapter IV: Lacan and Alterity

"Yes, talking to others makes me feel like sleeping. Only my ghostly and imaginary friends, only the conversations I have in my dreams, are genuinely real and substantial, and in them intelligence gleams like an image in a mirror."

Fernando Pessoa
"The Book of Disquiet" 2002, p. 48

Emerging from these studies of different approaches to alterity, I find that two theories provide durable and useful frameworks with which to "capture" the various forms of the phenomenon; the theories of Lacan and Dabrowski. For the time being I will not make the attempt to integrate these two theories. Instead, in this chapter and the next, I will briefly outline their essentials and show how the experience of alterity, in its several forms, can be usefully and interestingly described and explained in the terms of each of these theories.

These two theories survive to serve as useful "containers" for the concept of alterity because both admit of different forms of alterity. For Dabrowski, these occur along a developmental continuum. For Lacan they occur in different registers, or circuits of the Real, the Imaginary and the Symbolic. Ultimately, these can be reconciled, but that is perhaps a task for another day. First, let us turn to what might be a Lacanian account of alterity.

A: Circuits of Alterity

The work of Lacan (1977, 1981, 1993), although coming from a very different point of view from Dabrowski, offers an organizing framework for different types of alterity. I like to call these "circuits" of alterity to capture the fluidity and dynamism suggested by the Lacanian ideas that prompt these thoughts. It is important to note at the outset that while Dabrowski's scheme is developmental, Lacan rejects developmental schemes. Thus, we may see the three circuits of alterity I am proposing here as *phases* rather than *stages*, as *scenes* rather than *fixed locations*. What follows is not intended to be (nor could it be) an orthodox presentation of Lacanian ideas on alterity. Lacanian ideas are issued here as starting points (*points du capiton*) for further elaboration.

A good point of departure is Lacan's *schema L* (see also Evans, 1996).

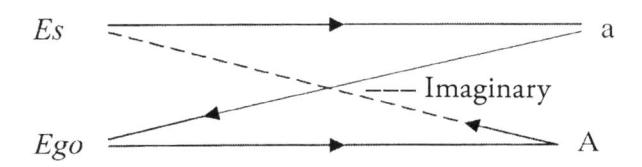

```
Es ─────────────────────→ a
      ╲         ╱
       ╲       ╱
        ╲ ╱── Imaginary
       ╱   ╲
      ╱     ╲
Ego ─────────────────────→ A
```

Figure 1: Schema L

Lacan created several versions of this scheme. The simplest is presented in the Figure 1 above. We may start with the *Es*, which may be understood roughly as the Freudian id. This stands in relationship to a (*l'objet petit a*, l'autre with small a) which is the other with small 'o'. This 'o' reflects the id and, in so doing, creates through its reflection by small a, the virtual image called the *Ego*. This ego, in its relations to the world, and especially in its relation to the paternal function and language, encounters a different form of the other, A, which is the big other, *l'objet grande A*. While *l'objet petit a* is reflective in its function, *l'objet grande A* is a rule-giving other. In this, it is the linked with the prohibiting, cutting off or castrating function of the paternal.

The final leg of the circuit is thus completed when *l'objet grand A* links back to the id (*Es*). Thus the Lacanian schema posits, as it were, two others--*a*, a reflective, imagination-saturated other and *A*, a law-giving other. Both others are influenced by the imaginary; *a*, because it is an object outside of the establishment of the symbolic which is established only in relation to *A*. *A* itself is suffused with the imaginary as is depicted in the line from *A* to *Es* as having to cross the line of the imaginary relation of *a* to ego.

I believe the *id-a* link is conceptually very close to the self-other link captured by Mahler's concept of symbiosis which, in turn, is similar to the mirroring "selfobject" of Kohut (1971, 1977). Relations with A, on the other hand, can be regarded as characteristic of more differentiated phases of development—for example Freud's oedipal stage or Mahler's rapprochement stage (1975).

In addition to Lacan's two objects, I also would suggest a third *objet*, *l'objet très grande A*. It seems that Lacan's schema L accounts for two domains of his famous Borromean Knot, namely the Imaginary and the Symbolic. It seems to ignore,

Alterity: The Experience of the Other

however, the register of the Real, the third circle in the knot.

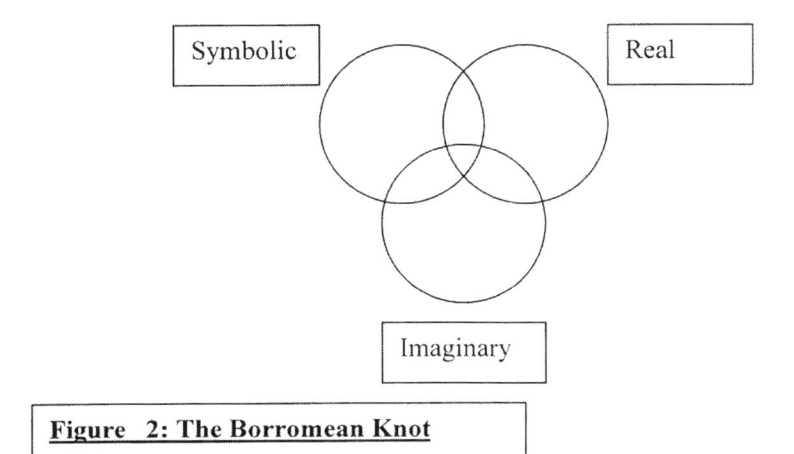

Figure 2: The Borromean Knot

I therefore propose the schema be extended to include the otherness of the third "Borromean domain," namely the Real. The Real thus provides a third form of alterity, a "third other." This third other includes, but is not coterminous with, the domain of nature. (It is unfortunate to note how little psychologists have examined the relationship of humans to the non-human environment. Searles (1979, 1960) provides an excellent exception).

The Lacanian schema thus can be extended. However, visualization of these three others in relation to the subject becomes exceedingly difficult if we are confined to static two dimensional space. Figure 3 is an attempt at pictorializing these three circuits of alterity.

Figure 3: Circuits of Alterity

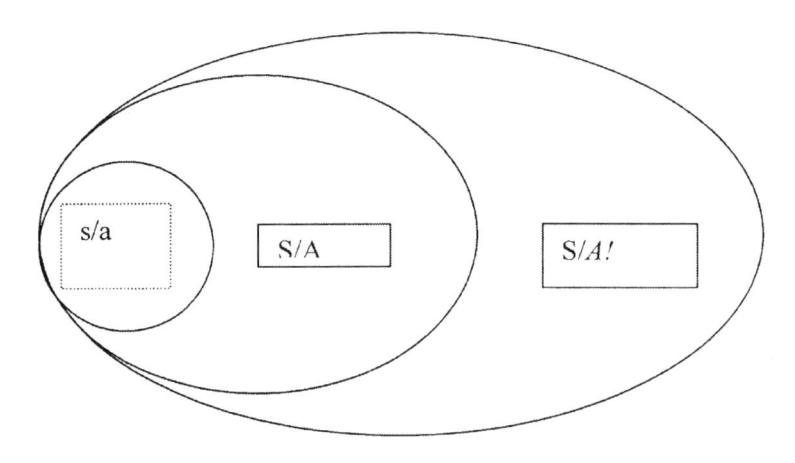

s/a corresponds to selfobject(Kohut)/symbiosis(Mahler) and is predominantly Imaginary

S/A corresponds to lawfulness of the Symbolic, the paternal function.

S/A! corresponds to the O of Bion and the Real of Lacan

Each loop is to be visualized as a moebius strip, giving the illusion of either two or one sidedness. Centers of subjectivity migrate from one circuit to another with great speed and with a "numbing sense of reality" (Bion, 1977) the oscillation in and amongst these circuits is continuous.

All three circuits operate simultaneously. However, attention is paid to where consciousness is directed at one or more circuits at any given time, depending on situational and personal variables. Thus,

Alterity: The Experience of the Other

individuals will focus from time to time and situation to situation on different circuits.

A few brief clinical vignettes may illustrate some possibilities of application.

Ray, a forty-seven-year-old single white man, currently residing in a long-term care nursing home and diagnosed with "delusional disorder" tells his therapist how, seven years ago, he was approached by several "entities" who informed him he was to be "arrested" in several days for the crimes he had committed. He was for the most part tormented and immobilized by these Kafkaesque entities, living a sequestered, uneventful life in the nursing home in which he resided. His personal history, at first blush, contained only one event of potential clinical importance, namely the sudden death of his father when he was seventeen. Every so often, in sessions, Ray would let on that he was at times puzzled by theses entities and that perhaps they were not "real." Perhaps they were imaginary. Perhaps they stood for something. Perhaps they were symbolic.

Using the template in Figure 3 to analyze Ray's predicament, we produce the following. Ray, for reasons as yet unascertained, felt guilty at the death of his father, as if he had broken the law. This violation, itself imaginary (we assume), was so powerful that he is trapped, as it were, in the Mobius strip of the imaginary *a* circuit.

Very little energy is devoted to the remaining circuits of A and *A!*. (His sequestered lifestyle reduces his contact with law, language and nature to the minimum). This configuration, this cathexis of the small *a* circuit is characteristic of what is called "delusion." His father's sudden death, the catastrophic failure of the Real of his father's body perhaps catapulted him back into the small *a* circuit. *A* and *A!* had proved too traumatic for him.

Psychotherapy, which opened up the possibilities, small at first, growing with time, of the symbolic meaning of these entities fires up, charges to an increasing degree, the large A circuit, which stands for the symbolic and the legalism of the symbolic systems. It also acknowledged *A!* the Real of his father's body. We were able to link *a*, *A* and *A!*, to link the Imaginary, Symbolic and the Real.

Six months later, Ray had a girlfriend, was no longer being visited by the entities and was entertaining the possibility of his moving out of the nursing home and into a group home. The oedipal strains in Ray's story are clear; what this schema brings to the fore, however, is the trend from cathexis of the small *a* circuit to the large *A* and the *A!* circuit involving relations with others that are symbolic and real, in this case, his girlfriend and the outside world.

B: The Phallic Organizer

The example of Ray above prompts the introduction of the concept of the "phallic organizer." The word organizer is used to deliberately evoke and connect with Spitz's concept of organizer, while at the same time connecting back to Lacan and the concept of alterity. Spitz's idea (1965) is that psychological development in the child is marked by a set of organizers (the social smile, object constancy, stranger anxiety) that both mark and catalyze a new psychological organization, a radically new gestalt. The idea here is that there exists a phallic organizer, that this organizer is similar in function to Lacan's "paternal function" and that this organizer, operating as it does across the domains of the Symbolic, Imaginary and the Real, plays a decisive role in the interplay of the three circuits of alterity just posited.

An anecdote may tie these ideas down to the ground. Jimmy is a teacher of math at junior college. Frequently when I talk to him about his teaching he will say of some of his students, "They need to snap out of it!" When I have seen those students, I have often been struck by the soft, sleepy, dreamy look in their eyes and I am reminded of Mahler's concept of "the hatched look," namely the look that comes into the baby's eyes as they enter the differentiation subphase and leave behind the drifting, dreaming fusion states of symbiosis. Many of his students seem not to have "the hatched look," Thus, I understand what Jimmy is talking about as some sort of "snapping out of" the symbiotic state, an awakening to circuits of alterity other than the dreamy thrall of the little *a*. This awakening is important for these students for several reasons. First, they are studying mathematics, an archetypal exemplar of the symbolic. If they remain in the little *a* circuit, they will not get math, at least not as a symbolic function, only as an imaginary function, for math involves cycling in the large *A* circuit. Second, they are learning mathematics ostensibly as part of the realization of a career trajectory or path. This will involve moving outward, leaving home, having adventures, encountering reality (*A*) and the Real (*A!*). Framed this way, I am led to concur with my friend Jimmy (who, by the way, has no psychodynamic training or interests) that "snapping out of it" might be a good idea. How does Jimmy try to get the students to snap out of it? He tells ribald jokes, often teasing the young men about their proclivities toward masturbation. He presents himself as a proud phallic male. He shows off. He gives surprises, sudden noises, jokes, quizzes. There is no sleep. He stands erect before the class unabashedly disporting his diplomas and qualifications. He rattles his keys and shows off his pinky ring. He makes more jokes about power struggles with his wife. He plays at being a very old fashioned, sexist male until people start to attack him. He teaches math too, and very successfully, and often teaches people who have long since given up the hope of ever passing a college math course.

Oftentimes, the young men who were deemed to be in need of "snapping out of it" become attached to Jimmy, as if he is very important to them. Viewed from the perspective being forwarded here, he is. He is performing the function of a phallic organizer, a totem around which the minds of these young people can organize themselves such that important dreams and aims can be realized. In the absence of such phallic organizers, behavior becomes *asymbolic*, the hermeneutic function described by Hazell (2003) erodes, perhaps collapses and neurosis, perhaps psychotic–like symptoms emerge.

Alterity: The Experience of the Other

We thus find an interesting parallel here to Lacan's ideas on the historical decline of paternalism, which is here read as a decline of the phallic organizing function. This is matched with a shift in the culture from old fashioned oedipal or conflict/drive neurotic symptoms to the more pervasive issues of personality disorders – problems of emptiness, will, identity and contact.

None of this is to be taken as an argument for a return to the patriarchal society; to do so would be to confuse the realms of the Imaginary, Symbolic and Real. The function of the phallic organizer when it operates in the Symbolic and Imaginary registers is as a social construction, a cultural artifact and an intrapsychic phenomenon. In the register of the Real, the phallic organizer is simply the penis. As Lacan informs us, many neurotic symptoms can be decoded as multiform games of "Where is the phallus?" each involving, to a greater or lesser extent, confusions as to the register in which the phallus exists; Symbolic, Imaginary or Real.

Similarly, Jimmy's attempts to get his students to "snap out of it" can be interpreted as stemming from his own phallic anxieties and a dread of regression to preoedipal dependency states. Not infrequently, people who are deeply depressed or agitated are told, inappropriately, to "snap out of it" or to develop a (phallic) "spine,"

Another example may further illustrate the concept of the phallic organizer. The code of Hammurabi is a code of laws from the ancient Mesopotamian civilization inscribed on a markedly phallic obelisk. Here we see social organization emanating from the paternal phallus inscribed on a phallic symbol. The symbolic function skirts the real so almost anyone could "get it." Viewed from a classical Freudian perspective, the obelisk symbolizes masculine pretensions of power. The Lacanian scheme argues that it is also a symbol of the symbolizing function itself, of laws, yes, but not only laws of the land, but also the laws of language, of the symbolic systems themselves.

Klein reminds us that, in the life of the mind, the phallus grows out of the breast and is deeply affected by pre-existing relations with the breast. Thus a bad breast will evolve with time into a bad phallus/breast and a good breast into a good phallus/breast. A good enough breast, a breast of the depressive position, will evolve into a good enough phallus. A split situation such as is found in the paranoid-schizoid position, will evolve into a split phallus, one good, one bad, and never the two shall meet.

These Kleinian ideas help explain the multiple forms of the phallic organizer—good, benevolent philosopher king, paranoid warlord, infantile, parasitic rulers and so on. For example, good enough mothering will create the stable image of the "good breast" and, as the concept of the phallus is differentiated with development, it joins with the matrix laid down by the good breast and it, along with everything it comes to stand for, becomes good or good enough. Thus, attitudes towards the symbolizing function (phallic) will rest upon relations to the breast, be they loving, hating, ambivalent, teasing, tormenting, confusing, ambivalent, split or integrated, to name only a few possibilities.

How is the concept of the phallic organizer so important in understanding phases of psychological development, related to the idea of alterity above and beyond the ways already intimated in this section? The phallic organizer comes to stand for alterity itself. The phallic symbol "sticks out." The root meaning of exist (*exigere*) means

Alterity: The Experience of the Other

to stick out. Thus, existence itself is symbolized by the phallus. This is yet another role of the phallic organizer, namely, to help codify, in a relatively stable form, the concepts, feelings, and fantasies associated with self-other differentiation.

Thus experiences of alterity will often be understood or spoken about in phallic ways. For example, in group analytic settings where the group experiences the radical alterity of the consultant, it may discuss this alterity in phallic forms, wondering, for example, about the consultant's "equipment" or "tackle" or "penetrating insights." The question often being posed in these discussions is what is the nature of the radical alterity of the consultant? Is it good, good enough, or bad? Does it represent a catastrophic alterity, such as we frequently find in the Real? Does it promise a symbiotic quasi alterity such as we find with the object with a small "o" *(l'objet petit a)*? We return to the question posed at the outset, "Where is the phallus?" only now with the question, "What is the phallus?"

In the last few paragraphs we have moved, willy-nilly, into the domain of the transference. The topic of transference has been touched on before in this effort but here these notions of circuits of alterity help organize some thoughts.

The transference can be understood as operating simultaneously, but with varying cathexes, through the three circuits of alterity, *a*, *A* and *A!*. When the therapist is the other as selfobject then the *a* circuit is activated. This would be the transferences, for example, described by Kohut—the mirroring, idealizing, merging and twinning transferences. When the therapist is experienced as the punisher, disciplinarian, tempter or boundary manager the circuit is often primarily that of

A. The therapist in these transference situations is the phallic Other. When the therapist is experienced as radically Other, the Other of the Real, this frequently involves experiences having to do with the body of the therapist and its Realness—its presence or absence, its aliveness or deadness, its qualities, smells, touch, health or procreative potential. Thus experiences involving these elemental components will activate the circuit of alterity *A!*—the circuit of radical alterity.

Trauma can often be understood as a rapid, unexpected shift from one circuit to another, often accompanied by an anxious feeling that return to the other circuits has been foreclosed. For example, a person involved in a symbiotic sentiment of oneness with another may be suddenly jarred from this (the small a circuit) into A when the other fails to respond with empathic resonance. They may be joined into the *A!* circuit by a sudden noise or the unforeseen departure or illness of the other.

In a reverse order, a person may be in the presence of another who is felt to be clearly other, a stranger, only to find themselves sliding into "falling in love" (which is the small *a* circuit), and while feeling pleasure, may also feel anxiety at the radical shift in alterity, of having the other move from "a stranger across a crowded room" to someone you know deeply and intimately, seemingly in a flash.

As a further illustration, we may use the epigraph of Don Miguel Ruiz, used at the very beginning of this book, in which he describes how he walked in the desert with a sense of nature's essential alterity (*A!*) which is radically transformed into a sense of unity with the cosmos (*a*). Don Miguel Ruiz is not traumatized by this, as we see in the first selection of epigraphs of this book, but sometimes people are. Freud

Alterity: The Experience of the Other

himself claimed not to understand the "oceanic sense" as described by Romain Rolland and many others deeply affected by this sense of oneness with the universe.

Perhaps individuals vary considerably in the ease with which they are able to shift operations from one circuit to another. In the very young, for example, the focus is largely on circuit *a*, with only a gradual expansion into *A* and *A!*. Experiences, both educational and traumatic, result in preferences for certain configurations or flows through these circuits. Some individuals remain firmly wedded to *A!* and eschew *a*, while others, for example, remain fixed in *a* and dislike *A* and *A!*. Yet others may be able to fluidly move from one circuit to another and be capable of exercising some control over their cathexes of these circuits.

Lacan rejects developmental paradigms. I share some of his suspicion of developmental schemes, for they often can be formulaic and can act as agendas given by those in position of privilege to those who are oppressed (Chodorow, 1989). Once these suspicions and risks have been "partialled out," however, certain developmental vectors still seem to remain. The Dabrowskian scheme (Chapter V) has, it seems, a good organizing potential with regard to a wide array of phenomena (Hazell, 2003, 2005a, b).

Thus, one might point a developmental line, not one that moves from *a* to *A* to *A!*, but one in which the individual is more capable of switching from *a* to *A* and *A!* with facility to the point where the individual is almost capable of appreciating the other simultaneously as existing in *a*, *A* and *A!*. It would be as if the individual would be able to say, with relative ease all at once, "You are part of me. You are Other than me. You are radically Other than me."

This position is very close to the position on alterity I posit for Levels IV and V of Dabrowski's scheme (Chapter V). At lower levels, especially level II, one finds the switching between the different circuits to be abrupt and sticky rather than smooth and flowing. In addition, the switching of circuits of alterity is not so much under conscious control (in Dabrowskian terms, not under the control of what he terms the "Third Factor") as it is at the higher levels.

As a result of this unexpected switching from one circuit of alterity to another at level II, often as a result of situational variables (recall that in the Dabrowskian scheme the 1st and 2nd Factors dominate behavior at the lower levels), the individual is confused. At one time they feel at one with the other (*a*); at another they feel separate *(A)*, at yet another they feel the other's radical alterity *(A!)*. They are thus buffeted from one sense of the other to another without any apparent rhyme or reason. Equally, they may find themselves "locked into" one of the circuits of alterity for an extended period of time and experience the pleasure and pains associated with each circuit. Locked into *a*, they live as if in symbiosis. Locked into A, they feel separate and cut off from others. Locked into A!, they experience a dreadful radical alienation from the world.

"Unexpected misfortune is always alteric" (Taussig, 1992). Thus, trauma, along with all the other developmental factors and features we can muster will have bearing on the outcomes along the developmental line of alterity. Trauma may precipitate and lock the individual into *A!*, perhaps with a desperate restitutive attempt to switch back into *a*, the circuit of alterity excluding *A!*. For example, this individual may immerse themselves in long periods of fantasy games or television. All this to no avail, until therapy or growthful experiences have restored an easier flow between the three circuits of alterity.

To conclude, it seems that an elaboration of certain Lacanian ideas into the notion that there are three circuits of alterity (a, A, $A!$) and that these three circuits correspond with Dabrowski's theoretical scheme has some organizing potential. This taxonomy of alterities brings order to the wide and variegated forms of alterity found in the literature. It seems theoretically consistent and can be empirically validated or refuted. A measure of alterity is under development at the time of going to press. Divisions of Dabrowski's theory can be measured. Thus research studies could be carried out to examine the validity and utility of these assertions. From an abstract and descriptive standpoint, it appears that there could possibly be a correspondence between the Dabrowskian levels and the ease with which one may move from one circuit to another versus the extent to which one is embedded in one circuit or the extent to which movement from one circuit to another is smooth and modulated by conscious control. The application of the Dabrowskian scheme to alterity will be more thoroughly examined in Chapter V.

C. Theorists Influenced by Lacan

Jean Laplanche:

Among psychoanalytic theorists influenced by Lacan, one of the most original and thought provoking responses to the problem of alterity is that of Jean Laplanche (1999). Key to Laplanche's response is the notion of *primal seduction*, an idea that posits the infant in the earliest stages of life being presented with an adult and the entire adult world. The infant is seduced in a primordial fashion by the adult's desires, language, symbols and behaviors. These are *implanted* in the relatively defenseless infant's mind where they become part and parcel of their unconsciousness. Thus it would seem that from the earliest eras of personal history there is a confusion regarding self and other. Much of what is deemed to be self results from primal seduction. The analyst is capable of acknowledging and "maintaining this dimension of inner alterity" (Laplanche, 1999, p. 228) and an aspect of the process of analysis is for the analysts themselves to unearth this "forcible entry" of the other into their unconscious.

Neurosis and the arrogance of psychosis, the certainty of the paranoiac and the racist rely upon the lack of acknowledgement of the radical alterity of the enigmatic originary other. The denial of this implanted other leads to denial of evidence of alterity, avoidance of enigma and this results in stasis and neurosis. Perhaps neurosis itself can be understood as ever-failing attempts at "the domestication of the otherness of the unconscious." (1999) However, Laplanche is quick to point out that "the unconscious (is) an internal other but not at the center." (1999) He is joining Lacan (at least here) in positing the decentered self/decentered other. The drives, however are drives emanating from the subject-object scene of primal seduction.

The transference for Laplanche thus has two forms: *le transfert en plein* (in full) and *le transfert en creux* (hollowed out). The transference in full relates to misconceptions of the analyst (or other) resulting from repressed and then projected childhood memories. The hollowed out transference has to do with "the emergence of the enigmatic originary other of prehistory." In this the lines drawn around alterity radically shift, for "to allow an enigma is to allow alterity. The enigma leads back, then, to the otherness of the other." (Laplanche 1999, p.255)

Laplanche, in addition, draws proactive connections between the establishment of time (and afterwardness) and alterity.

> *"The stone has an excess of world, the living being cuts off from excess of world precisely in order to establish time for itself. There is no perception and no memory (even immediate) without something constituting itself as a separate organism, in active retrenchment from the world."*
> *(1999. p. 239-40)*

It would thus appear that Laplanche is connecting the development of a certain sense of time with the establishment of self-other boundaries. Clearly, since the sense of time is so crucial to other concepts (history, causality, futurity, narrative, etc.), the sense of alterity and its vicissitudes stand in a position of radical importance.

Laplanche clearly stands in opposition to the concept of primary autism, for the situation of primary seduction is a self-other situation, one where the infant asks (in our imaginations) "What does the breast want from me?" The desire of the other as well as the desire for the other thus forms a nucleus for what later will be called the self.

Laplanche, in reformulating Freud's abandoned seduction theory and following post-modern psychoanalytic thinkers' explorations of the "radical decentering of the human psyche," causes us to ponder deeply before rapidly coming to conclusions on the nature of alterity.

Rosine Lefort:

Rosine Lefort, in , "The Birth of the Other," (1994) presents two case studies of psychotherapeutic work she did with two young girls, Nadia, aged thirteen and a half months and Marie-Francoise, who was thirty months old when Lefort commenced treatment. Lefort's presentation is in and of itself interesting insofar as she presents the process notes she wrote at the time of the treatment and follows these with a retrospective analysis along Lacanian lines, thus giving an interesting "double" image of the process.

It is quite beyond my reach and intent here to fully react to this monumental piece of work. I will simply address certain themes which chime with those under investigation here. Of especial interest to most American psychologists, steeped as they frequently are in the Mahlerian scheme of separation-individuation, is to have data presented on two young girls that would ordinarily be interpreted as "differentiation" or "normal autism" spoken of in the language of Lacanian theory. It is a real eye-opener. The two streams of interpretation enrich our understanding of these troubled children. Both little girls have been terribly traumatized. They have been repeatedly abandoned and they are both very ill and under extreme stress. In Mahlerian terms we would say that the process of separation and differentiation has been derailed and there is need of support to help growth towards self and object constancy and the establishment of a sense of individuality. In the Lacanian framework, the establishment of the other (with a small o) and the Other (with a big O) have been held up. Consequently the child is trapped in the Real and is unable to symbolize themselves as a subject and the other as an Object. Nadia, for example, is trapped in "the pure Real of bodies" where she is "handled without being spoken" (p. 6).

Lefort charts the deep, complex and oftentimes circuitous pathways whereby the senses of self and other are established, quite decisively for Nadia, less completely so for Marie-Francoise, for whom the story is left unfinished.

Several threads help map out these tortuous pathways. First, Lefort documents the child's use of *separable objects* in their relation to the other. The separable object seems to signify that the other can lack something, for example when Nadia takes off Lefort's glasses and throws them away. If this is the case, that the object can lack something, so the reasoning goes, then the object must be have a finite surface, must be bounded, must have or not have contents. The object becomes a "holed other," thus separate. Lefort presents a tantalizing theory (that meshes beautifully with Mahlerian ideas) that in early infancy there is exclusively a conception of subjectivity as a *mobius strip,* a strip folded in on itself in such a way that it only has one surface. This is a topological way of conceptualizing the pre-objectal state—the state before alterity in either small or grande "a" form. When the infant realizes that the other has a lack, is missing something, this conception is disrupted and the object is seen as a *torus,* basically as a doughnut shape. There is a hole in the middle. The surface is unbounded but it is not infinite. Now the child conceives of a subject and a separate object…at first it is the object with the small "o". This in turn is linked with the concept of envy or *invidia* as Lefort calls it. She observes that when she touches the crib of another child, Nadia has an envious fit, this arising from the realization that the other has an other and in the fact that "for the first time Nadia encountered an adult who could lack a small other."

Separable objects are also important indicators for Lefort, of the shift from *metaphor* to *metonymy*. Metaphor, Lefort argues involves the substitution of an entire object for another as in for example: My Uncle: A Leech. Metonymy, on the other hand, substitutes an element of the object for the object as in, for example, My Uncle: Bad Breath. Both are symbolic constructions, but, argues Lefort, Metonymy is more sophisticated and later to develop than metaphor. Metonymy, in its economy, is closer to symbolic language. Metonymy develops out of the child's usage of the object's separable and non-separable parts. We thus see in the development of both children the development of language as they play with, tear off and throw away or attempt to throw away the separable and non-separable parts of Lefort as she interacts with them. Lefort establishes conditions in which metaphor and metonymy could operate and interprets the children's activities accordingly. Lefort reports that, "the use of the signifier 'Mama' put the seal on the difference between her and me."

Alterity is established along auditory and visual lines. When, for example, Nadia hears her voice called by the other and when she sees herself being held by Lefort in the reflection of the mirror. In fact, it seems that Lefort posits a "pre specular phase" in the development of alterity, sharing with us her impression that Nadia was in a sense reborn when she encountered her image in the mirror. The mirror, of course, is significant in Lacanian theory. Lefort points out again the symbolizing function of the mirror insofar as we encounter in the mirror the Real of our body, as it is captured in a virtual image-space "behind" the mirror through the use of the "symbolizing surface of the mirror itself." The mirror serves as a concrete representation of the symbolizing function.

When Lefort turns her attention to Marie-Francoise, we witness a little girl who is more deeply disturbed, for, "Neither the Other nor the other were present for Marie Francoise." Marie Francoise had suffered deeper and more extended trauma in her life, so once again we find disruptions in the senses of alterity corresponding with intensity of experienced trauma. So deep was Marie-Francoise's withdrawal from the world that she would suffer convulsions in front of food—evincing intense suffering in front of the desired object. It appeared that Marie-Francoise could not tolerate an "other" in her world. Lefort interprets therefore that when Marie Francoise sticks objects up against her eyes, or presses them against her face, that she is attempting to erase the boundaries between herself and the other, to make herself and the object both seamless parts of an unbounded Real. Lefort also notices that Marie Francoise was prone to using a, "schizophrenic defense, aimed at a reduction of my person to a livable-with other." Thus, Marie Francoise would try to poke a spoon into her eye and Lefort interprets, "I was an Other for which she had a need, which she searched for, but to which she could not address any demand because that Other was not the holder of a separable object." We see that in this, Marie Francoise has farther to travel than Nadia, who was capable of relating to separable parts of the Other. Also indicative of Marie-Francoise's deeper distress is the fact that she evinced no signs of *invidia*, to which Lefort interprets, "Without the Other, there is no *invidia* or jealousy but only isolated sadistic drive." This strikes one as a telling depiction of profound mental agony. Much of the work with Marie-Francoise seemed to focus on concepts of container and contained. She was interested in the inside of pots and cups, as if the concept of contents is essential to the formation of the concept of the other. Once again invoking concepts from topology, Lefort notes, "She had a body in the form of a torus without having passed through the body structure of the mobius strip." Marie-Francoise, from a Mahlerian viewpoint would perhaps have been analyzed as a child whose passage from Normal Autism into Symbiosis had been thwarted. Lefort's analysis, along Lacanian lines offers a fascinating and tantalizing alternative line of interpretation.

Chapter V: TPD: An Integrative Framework

"I is an other—don't let this impress you! Don't start spreading it around that I is an other—it won't impress anyone, believe me! And what is more it doesn't mean anything. Because, to begin with, you have to know what an other means. The other—don't use this term as mouthwash."

(Lacan, Seminar Book II, p. 7)

Clive Hazell

Introduction: The Theory of Positive Disintegration and Alterity

Many of the phenomena we encounter in examining alterity can be usefully explained and organized when we apply the concepts, ideas and hypotheses of Kazimierz Dabrowski's theory of emotional development, the theory of positive disintegration.

I have used this theory, in my other books, to explain other phenomena, for example, group processes and the experience of emptiness. In this chapter, I will give a brief description of the theory of positive disintegration (the same one used in my other books, *The Experience of Emptiness,* and *Imaginary Groups*). Then we will examine several of the ideas in the theory as they can be applied to explain and organize the concept of alterity. The theory of positive disintegration, or aspects of it, is delineated in a number of volumes including Dabrowski, Kawczak and Piechowski (1970) and Dabrowski and Piechowski (1977).

The theory of positive disintegration (TPD) states that there are five hierarchically organized levels of development. The process of development involves a transcending of an earlier structure through its disintegration and ultimate restructuring into a new structure. Thus, disintegration is seen as positive, as being a necessary process for development to occur. One of Dabrowski's books is entitled *Psychoneurosis is Not a Disease.* In it, he argues that many things that are understood as "neurotic" are, in fact, breakdown phenomena resulting from emotional development; they are signs that psychological growth is occurring.

We can see that alterity exists at multiple levels: biological, intrapsychic, interpersonal, group, institutional, cultural, societal, political and global. We can use the theory of positive disintegration of Kazimierz Dabrowski (1970, 1977) as an organizing framework for all the previously described conceptions of alterity. Thus, the different conceptions of alterity will be placed on a developmental continuum that corresponds to the levels of Dabrowski's theory.

It is important to note, however, that these placements are not entirely diachronic. That is, forms of alterity do not map in a rigid one-to-one fashion for levels of TPD. Since TPD is an hierarchical theory, there will be considerable synchronic aspects to this matching. All levels are present, to a greater or lesser degree, and with greater or lesser degrees of realization in every individual. Thus, for example, while a level III individual will manifest "level III type alterities," one will also find evidence of alterities typical of all the other levels, although to a lesser degree. In fact, it is the very presence of these different levels within the individual (or within the group) that potentiate development, giving, for example, glimpses of possibilities for further emotional development.

The methodology here is the same as that found in *The Experience of Emptiness* (Hazell 2003) where different forms of the experience of emptiness were shown to be yoked to different levels in TPD.

Clive Hazell

The Theory of Positive Disintegration

The Levels of Development

<u>Level I - Primary Integration</u>:

At this level the person is organized around the meeting of basic survival needs. The person at this stage feels relatively well integrated, and has as his primary purpose the meeting of "instinctual needs," e.g. hunger, sex, safety, shelter, comfort. It seems as though the person is dealing primarily with what Maslow (1968) termed "basic needs" and not "meta-needs," or higher level needs. The individual at this level of development is unaware of meta-needs, or if he is aware of them, assimilates them to his or her primary orientation of meeting basic needs. This would occur in much the same fashion that Kohlberg (1976) has demonstrated that people of lower levels of moral development interpret and assimilate the acts of higher moral development entirely in the terms of lower moral development. That is, for example, they may interpret altruistic acts as being acts of meeting basic needs. Level I is the level of the confident, unconflicted, self-serving individual. They are untroubled by a conscience or concern for others.

<u>Level II - Unilevel Disintegration</u>:

At this level the relatively smooth functioning of Level I breaks up, disintegrates and leaves the person with a predominantly wavering attitude. The previously well-bound and integrated structure now becomes loose, resulting in the individual feeling attacks of directionlessness and chaos. There is a difficulty in making decisions; forces within the person push against one another so that the person vacillates. In the absence of an internal hierarchical organization (the disintegration is unilevel) the forces do not resolve into smooth and deliberate action. The person at this stage is very subject to polarities of emotion. Sometimes the disintegration can be extreme and result in substance abuse or even psychosis. In other instances, the person can "pull themselves together" and manage to function in a seemingly integrated way. Under pressure, however, the disintegration returns. Frequently people at this stage long for a return to the "good old days" of Primary Integration, when things seemed, by comparison, simple. The words of Yeats' poem (1989) seem to capture Unilevel Disintegration quite aptly:

> *"Things fall apart, the center cannot hold,*
> *Mere anarchy is loosed upon the world."*

The hallmarks of this level are other-directedness, ambivalence, mixed feelings, ambitendency, confused and conflictual activity, and the sense of having multiple selves. The individual is unsure as to what is really important, as to what should take precedence.

Level III - Spontaneous Multilevel Disintegration:

At this level of development, things are still fallen apart, but there is a growing hierarchization within the person. Instead of equipotent forces acting upon each other, resulting in a wavering, vacillating directionlessness, there is a developing sense of a hierarchy of values, with certain values and forces emerging as prepotent. The person begins to feel "inferiority towards himself," that is, he starts to experience the difference between what he is and what he ought to be. This develops out of the newly-emerging hierarchy of aims and values. Among some of the other "dynamisms" (or experiences that can facilitate and encourage further development) are: positive maladjustment, feelings of guilt, feelings of shame, astonishment with oneself, hierarchization, subject-object in oneself, inner psychic transformation and self-awareness, self-control, autopsychotherapy and education-of-oneself.

Level IV - Organized Multilevel Disintegration:

In this stage the person has developed an organized and consistent hierarchy within him or herself. In the words of Ogburn (1976):

> *"He has transcended the problem of becoming*
> *And tackles the problems of being." (Ogburn, 1976)*

The basic needs are generally well taken care of at this stage or have receded into the background; the individual is concerned largely with the meta-needs that Maslow speaks of. (Maslow, 1968, p. 210) In fact, Piechowski (1982) argues that there is a strong correspondence between the Self Actualizing person of Maslow's thinking and the person who has achieved Level IV. Thus, some of the active dynamisms are: self-awareness, knowledge of one's uniqueness, developmental needs, existential responsibility, self-control, regulating one's own development, education-of-oneself, self-induced programs of systematic development. The primary task of the individual at this stage of development is to solidify the structure that emerges from the previous disintegrated stage.

The locus of control (that is, whether they feel they are directed from within themselves or without) for the individual at Level IV is very firmly an internal one. He or she can act independently of the external environment if he so chooses.

Level V – Secondary Integration:

Only a few rare individuals reach this level of development. At this stage, the "ought" has become unified with "what is." The personality ideal has been achieved. The planful self-development of Level IV has been successfully completed. Individuals at this level seem to experience self, other, time, being and the world in radically different ways. Thus, persons at the other levels often have difficulty understanding them.

Overexcitabilities

Development through the stages is related, in large part, to the level and profile of excitabilities in the person. Dabrowski posits five types of overexcitabilities: Emotional, Psychomotor, Sensual, Intellectual and Imaginational. An overexcitability is a predisposition in the individual, largely inherited, to respond to certain types of stimuli in an above average manner. For example, a person with sensual overexcitability will be more responsive than average to cutaneous stimulation. He or she will also tend, if this tends to be his or her dominant type of overexcitability, to transform other types of experience, (e.g., emotional, intellectual, imaginational) into sensual types of experience. For example, the emotion of affection will be readily transformed into stroking for a person with sensual overexcitability.

Perhaps another term for overexcitability would be sensitivity, perhaps analogous to photographic paper which can be varied in its sensitivity to various types of light input. The pronounced overexcitability would correspond to a finely grained, highly sensitized paper, the impression of reality gained when there is an overexcitability that is correspondingly sharp, intense and vivid.

Following is a brief overview of the manifestations of the various forms of overexcitabilities (OEs):

Sensual: This manifests through a heightened sensitivity to sensual experience—skin stimulation, sexual excitability, the desire for stroking, physical comfort, tastes, sights, colors, etc.

Psychomotor: This manifests itself in a tendency for vigorous movement, violent games and sports, rapid talk and a pressure to be moving. Emotional excitement is converted into movement that is highly charged with energy. Dancers and athletes might have a high degree of this OE.

Imaginational: This is shown in sensitivity to the imagined possibilities of things. There is a rich association of images and metaphors flow freely. People with high levels of this OE might easily confuse reality and imagination.

Intellectual: In this the individual displays a voracious curiosity and desire to learn and understand. There is a persistence in asking probing questions and a reverence for logic. There is a love of theory and an intense enjoyment of thinking.

Emotional: This is the most important overexcitability in that if this is absent or weak, it is unlikely that development will proceed. Emotional overexcitability is manifested in the person's ability to form strong emotional attachments to others, and living things and places. Also present with emotional overexcitability are: concern about death, strong affective memory, concern for others, empathy, exclusive relationships and feelings of loneliness. People with high levels of this OE often say they are "too emotional."

The level of development the individual reaches is dependent upon three factors. The first factor is the person's hereditary endowment, namely, the configuration of his overexcitabilities and other genetic inheritances. The second factor is the environment in which the individual lives and the extent to which it supports or impedes that individual's development, for example, family, school, community. The third factor consists of the individual's response to his or her situation—the decisions he or she makes in response to the life situation they find themselves in and the genetic heritage that they possess.

The third factor is only found significantly at Level III or above, that is, persons at levels I and II are molded entirely by genetic, constitutional and environmental factors. Only at Level III does the individual start to take hold of his or her situation (in an almost "existential" way) and make a conscious, self-determined choice as to how they will act.

Equipped with this brief overview of TPD let us now examine how the multiple forms of alterity correspond with the different levels of Dabrowski's theory.

Correspondences of Forms of Alterity with Levels of TPD

Figure 4 provides an image of the correspondence of notions of alterity to levels in the theory of positive disintegration.

Figure 4: Correspondences of Alterity and TPD

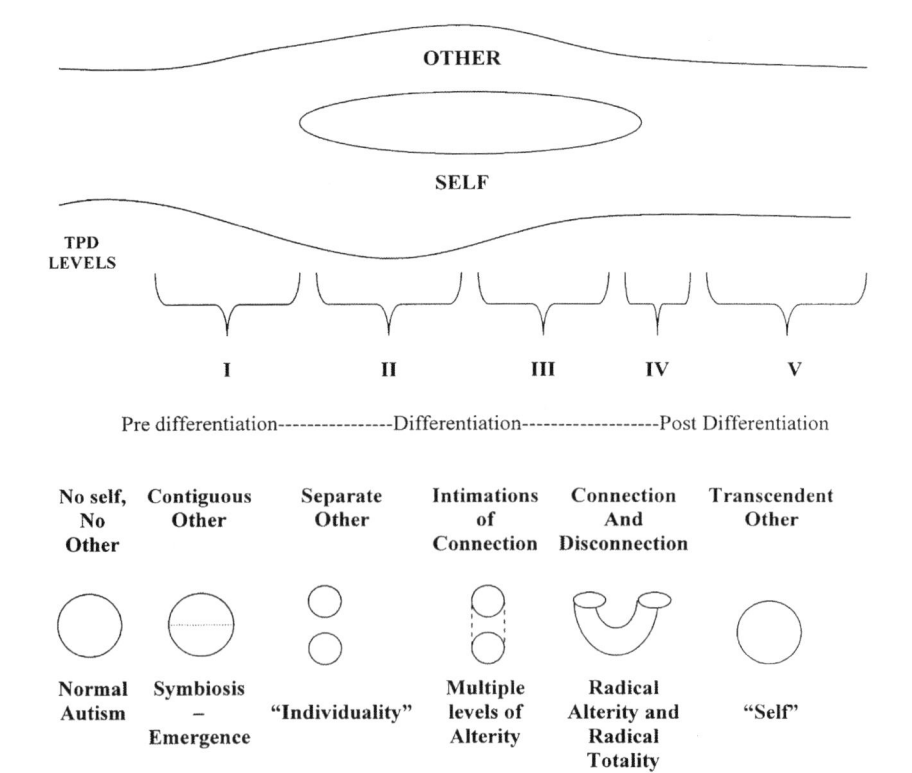

OTHER

SELF

TPD LEVELS

I II III IV V

Pre differentiation----------------Differentiation-------------------Post Differentiation

No self, No Other	Contiguous Other	Separate Other	Intimations of Connection	Connection And Disconnection	Transcendent Other
Normal Autism	Symbiosis – Emergence	"Individuality"	Multiple levels of Alterity	Radical Alterity and Radical Totality	"Self"

The diagram attempts to show the correspondences between the levels of TPD and different forms of alterity. Development proceeds from left to right, from level I to V. As this development takes place so the sense of self and other is altered. This course of development is also consonant with that posited by Miller (2008).

The developmental process is both diachronic and synchronic, especially in terms of alterity. It is diachronic insofar as there is a linear progression, through time, and if development occurs, from lower levels to higher levels. However, it is also synchronic insofar as once a higher level has been reached, the individual has the capacity to "regress" to or to access earlier forms of alterity (for example, in sleep) and also contains synchronous representations of alternative notions of self and other in both the conscious and unconscious mind. Synchronic elements are also present in the model insofar as the potential for later forms of alterity are also present and, to a greater or lesser extent, ready to be activated in the individual at relatively lower levels of development.

Level I corresponds with forms of alterity that exist before differentiation of self and other, as we find in Mahler's concept of "normal autism." As development proceeds toward self-other differentiation, concepts of self and other progress through "symbiosis" (Mahler, 1975) and the "contiguous other" (Ogden 1983). Prior to the emergence of these concepts of self and other we find the "sensation shapes" of Tustin (1972, 1990).

Level II is ushered in by concepts of self and other that are still dominated by sensory impressions and physical experiences. Since the majority of people are at level II, these ideas of self and other are very common and conventional, rarely being questioned by most people. It is as if most people, operating at this level, adopt the position, "I am me; you are you. We are separate. It's only common sense." In fact, this stage could perhaps be labeled the stage of the conventional, common sense self.

As individuals progress through this stage, the apparent stability begins to break up. For one thing, going along with the crowd, and its many voices, is not so easy. Secondly, the individual becomes more aware of their many internal selves. By extension, there is a dawning awareness that others have multiple selves. In this, and in communication, there is some sense of connection of self and other.

The person at level II, often feels isolated. Self is separate from other, sustained, perhaps by "object constancy" but lacking any deep connection with the other, save in regressions to "symbiosis." The otherness of the other at this stage can thus often involve a painful, sometimes terrifying aloneness. Most psychology belongs to this level of development in that it operates on notions of separate monistic selves and others.

At Level III hierarchization of parts of the self occur and fleeting intimations of a deeper, more continuous self-other connectedness occur. These intimations of connection are different from symbiosis and the individual has much work to do to separate these two types of experience. In addition, these intimations of self-other connection are unconventional and this throws the person into a condition of "positive maladjustment," of not fitting in with society by virtue of the activation of higher order, and rarer functions.

Level III is quite confusional so these different experiences of self and other, self with other, self as other require much thinking out and this consumes much time and effort. Much existential psychology fits at this level.

At Level IV we find this psychological effort has paid off and the intimations of a "transcendent" self-other unity have become stabilized and organized. There is still "self" and still "other" but these are connected in a deeper fashion. Thus, in the Level IV person we find an unconventional notion of self and other and individual responsibility—ideas different from the norm—ideas often found in poetry, speeches of inspired leaders, gurus and some psychologists.

Jung's theory, with it concepts of the collective unconscious and synchronicity, provides ideas congruent with this level of development, as do notions from Lacan, Laplanche, Merleau-Ponty and especially Levinas.

Level V, the level of secondary integration, goes beyond words. At this level the concepts of self and other are fused into one. This level is hardly ever addressed in psychology, perhaps because Level V moves beyond conventional meanings of the concepts of "self" and "other." No psychological language has been developed for this domain. Furthermore, such a domain seems somehow unscientific and perhaps psychologists, anxious to preserve their image as "scientific" in the conventional sense of the word, have been reluctant to venture into this area. Philosophers and theologians, perhaps because they are unhampered by such concerns, have ventured here. Perhaps Hegel's (and Kojève's) "absolute master" is Level V. Perhaps the mystery of the other, written about by Levinas (1969, 1987, 2000, 2006) refers to level V experiences. The *Upanishads* and many other religious writings are filled with references to such forms of self-other experiences, references that are often hard for persons at Levels I-IV to decode.

We can see, therefore, that there are correspondences between TPD and the multiple forms of alterity that seem to exist. TPD provides an organizing framework for all of these experiences. It is therefore my contention that an extremely useful order can be brought to the many forms of alterity by utilizing TPD. Each and every one of the forms discussed in this text can be placed at a range along the developmental levels of this theory. We thus end up with a "geography" of alterity which can provide us with serviceable maps in many arenas.

Chapter VI: Where is the Object?

Where is the object? This question is answered too quickly by most psychologists.

The Mahlerian scheme does not (seem to) broach the topic, assuming fairly conventional models of inner and outer. The object in this scheme is ultimately found outside, beyond the subject and represented *inside* the subject.

The boundaries, or margins, become blurred when we introduce interpersonal defense mechanisms of introjection, projection, projective identification, insofar as subject and object get mixed up, but this mixing is a mixing *from* a prior state of separation. The state of separation is the reality to which the healthy return.

The door is still left open to the possibility that the question "Where is the object?" has just been answered by the baby and by the child psychologists. So the theory of the theory might be accurate but do we have to stop there?

This is perhaps where the philosopher takes over. The phenomenology of the philosopher is different perhaps from the phenomenology of the toddler. Thus, there can be multiple theories of self and other. Perhaps alterity (separation/individuation) develops *beyond* that posited by Mahler. Mahler's end point is self/other differentiation. This end point is offered as an "on the way to…" but has tended to be taken up as the Real of self-other differentiation.

Psychotherapy will help the individual reclaim projected parts and disown introjections and identifications and redefine self-other boundaries, and this, again, is towards conventional self-other boundaries. These conventional self-other boundaries are functional in the current social, economic and legal environment. It is consistent with current social, economic, legal and ethical ideas regarding individual responsibility. Thus, pragmatically, there is an available answer to the question, "Where is the object?" But it is only *an* answer and other answers exist. Perhaps these answers lie on a developmental continuum or cycle. Perhaps these answers exist in a cognitive space.

This book can be seen as an attempt to map out different conceptions of alterity. These conceptions will always leave the ultimate answer open, will leave the question "Where is the object?" still hanging. One of the contentions of this work is that the question should be left open, that the nature of alterity is a domain of exploration, perhaps, a very important one and that to close it off prematurely is to close off vital realms of social and psychological development.

Conventional wisdom regarding alterity has pragmatic value given current social and economic realities. If these realities do change or are to be changed, perhaps different notions of self and other would have pragmatic value.

This pragmatic/phenomenological approach liberates us to explore different models of alterity, suspending, at least for the time being, any questions of their correspondence to ultimate reality. What follows are descriptions of (several) (N) conceptions of alterity.

These conceptions are organized into an overarching developmental cycle. This cycle commences with the Mahlerian scheme and progresses through adolescence into adulthood and old age. Broadly, this scheme posits that the first half of life is directed toward the establishment of conventional self-other differentiation such that functioning in the current social-economic matrix is established.

Subsequently, in the second half of life this model of alterity is revamped (if development is to proceed). After midlife notions of self and other are deeply transformed to a state that might be called "paradoxical alterity"—a state where while separation of self and other is recognized, deep fusions between self and other are also recognized. These developments have been described by many other writers. They have not, however, been integrated into an overarching developmental scheme, nor have attempts been made to measure (and psychologize) these often philosophical concepts. The overall drift and conception of this theory is in line with Dabrowski's theory of positive disintegration, and these correspondences have been explored in this work.

Appendix: Alterity and Emptiness

I have described and provided an explanation for the experience of emptiness in Hazell (2003). The experience of emptiness was argued to be correlated with the sequence of emotional development described by Dabrowski (1970, 1977). I argue in this study that alterity, too corresponds in its various forms to the Dabrowskian levels (see chapter V). The experience of emptiness and alterity are thus interconnected. It is the aim of this section to highlight some of these relationships.

At Level 1 of Dabrowski's scheme the experience of emptiness is uncommon. Individuals at this level successfully keep this experience at bay with their absence of sustained introspection, concreteness, and tendency to act out rather than entertain new thoughts. This corresponds to an unreadiness to apprehend the other as radically other. The other is subsumed into the self, not subsumed in such a way as to promote empathy, for this implies an independently existing (mysterious) other, but subsumed in a primordial way, a way that blots out the possibility of another.

As the individual progresses towards Level II, self other differentiation increases. This differentiation creates a space between self and other. This space is one of the origins of the experience of emptiness. The emptiness persists and becomes painful if the individual is not able to fill it with transitional phenomena (to use Winnicott's term). In turn, individuals may respond to this psychic pain with all kinds of acting out. Thus the increase in separation and differentiation and its attendant sense of alterity precipitates the experience of emptiness. One way to blot out the emptiness, therefore, is to reduce, or obliterate the sense of otherness of the other.

Conversely, one way to stimulate the experience of emptiness is to introduce an experience that stimulates the experience of otherness. Interestingly, since the process of learning, especially learning from experience, involves the acquaintance with radical alterity in the form of an experience that falls beyond one's current span of personal knowledge, the experience of emptiness will be part and parcel of the growth process. This may help explain the resistance to learning, especially learning from experience, that any teachers, trainers or therapists frequently experience.

Viewed from this perspective, it can be surmised that the experience of alterity, besides shaking ones sense of narcissistic completeness and omniscience, undermines one's sense of power, control and competence. Here, in the other, is evidence that one is not all, not all knowing, not all-powerful. One is, momentarily at least, powerless. Again, one can react to this by regressing to a denial of difference by the attendant creation of pseudo differences. These operate as neurotic compromises between the recognition of and the fear of alterity. For example, one "learns about" something rather than learns from experiencing something. Thus one can say to the world and oneself, I have learned this, I have taken a course, when in reality all that has taken place is a carefully and elaborately disguised process of <u>assimilation</u> in the Piagetian sense of the word.

References And Bibliography

Abbott, E, 2008, *Flatland*, BiblioLife.

Adorno, T., 2006, *The Jargon of Authenticity*, Routledge, London.

Allport, G., 1955, *Becoming, Basic Considerations for a Psychology of Personality*, Yale, New Haven, CT.

Badiou, A., 2005, *Infinite Thought: Truth and the Return to Philosophy*. Continuum.

Bandura, A. and Walters, R. 1963, *Social Learning and Personality Development*, Holt, Rinehart and Winston.

Bataille, G., 1991, *The Accursed Share: Volume 1, Consumption*. Zone Books.

Baudrillard, J. and Guillaume, M. 2008, *Radical Alterity*, Semiotexte, Los Angeles, CA.

_____, 1995, *Simulacra and Simulation*, University of Michigan Press.

Beck, A., Freeman, A. and Davis, D., *Cognitive Therapy of Personality Disorders, Second Edition,* Guilford Press.

Beckett, S. 1966, *Molloy, Malone Dies, The Unnamable, Three Novels,* Calder and Boyars, London.

_____, 1958, *Endgame,* Grove Press, New York.

_____, 1966, *En Attendant Godot,* Editions de Minuit, Paris.

Benjamin, W., 2002, *The Arcades Project,* Belknap Press.

Berger, P. and Luckmann, T., 1991, *The Social Construction of Reality,* Penguin, London.

Bion, W. 1959, "Attacks on Linking," *Second Thoughts,* London, Heinemann (1967)

_____, 1961, *Experiences in Groups,* London, Tavistock.

_____, 1977, *Seven Servants,* New York, Jason Aronson.

_____, 1997, *Taming Wild Thoughts,* Karnac, London.

_____. 1987, *Clinical Seminars and Four Papers,* Fleetwood, Abingdon.

Blos, P., 1985, *Son and Father, Before and Beyond the Oedipus Complex,* Free Press.

Bollas, C. 1987, *The Shadow of the Object,* Columbia University Press, NY.

Bowen, M. 1994, *Family Therapy in Clinical Practice* Jason Aronson, New York.

Bowlby, J., 1980, *Loss,* Basic Books, New York.

Brin, D., 1994, *Otherness,* Bantam, New York.

Buber, M. (1958) *I and Thou.* New York, Scribners.

Camus, A., 1965, *Le Mythe de Sysyphe,* Gallimard, Paris.

_____, 1942, *L'Etranger,* Gallimard, Paris.

Carrier, J., 1995, *De Los Otros,* Columbia University Press.

Chodorow, N., 1989, *Feminism and Psychoanalytic Theory,* ale, New Haven.

Cohen, R. 2006, Introduction: Humanism and Anti Humanism—Levinas, Cassirer and Heidegger, *in Humanism of the Other* (Levinas 2006)

Coleridge, S. T., 1827, *Specimens of the Table Talk,* Kessinger, London

Colman, A.D. and Bexton, W.H. (eds) 1975, *Group Relations Reader,* Washington, DC, A.K. Rice Institute.

Colman, A.D. and Geller, W.H. (eds) 1985), *Group Relations Reader 2,* Washington, DC, A.K. Rice Institute.

Conrad, J. 1993, *The Secret Sharer,* Dover Publications.

Correia, E. 2005, Alterity and Psychotherapy, *Existential Analysis,* 16, 1, January

Dabrowski, K. and Piechowski, M.M., 1977 *Theory of Emotional Development,* Dabor, Oceanside, New York.

Dabrowski, K., Kawczak, A., Piechowski, M., 1970, *Mental Growth through Positive Disintegration*, Gryf, London.

Dabrowski, K. and Piechowski, M. M., 1977, *Theory of Emotional Development*, Dabor, Oceanside, NY.

Daruna, J. 2004, *Introduction to Psychoneuroimmunology*, Elsevier, Burlington, MA.

De Beauvoir, S. 1993, *The Second Sex*, Everyman's Library.

Derrida, J., 2007, *Psyche, Inventions of the Other*, Stanford University Press, Stanford, CA.

de Sa Carneiro, M., 1914, *Dispercao*, (cited in, Saraiva, A. J. ,1997, *Initiation into Portuguese Literature*, University of California, Santa Barbara, CA.

Dewey, John, 1998, *The Essential Dewey: Ethics, Logic, Psychology*. Indiana University Press.

A Dictionary of Psychology, 2009, Colman, A. Oxford Paperback Reference.

DSM IV, 1994, *Diagnostic and Statistical Manual of Mental Disorders*, Fourth Edition, American Psychiatric Association, Washington, D.C.

Dollard, J. and Miller, N., 1950, *Personality and Psychotherapy*, McGraw-Hill.

Donne, J., 1624, *Devotions Upon Emergent Occasions, Meditation 17*, in Complete Poetry and Selected Prose of John Donne, John Hayward (ed), 1929.

Dueck, A. and Parsons, T. 2007, Ethics, Alterity and Psychotherapy: a Levinasian approach, *Pastoral Psychology,* 55: 271-282.

Durkheim, E. 1951, *Suicide,* Free Press, New York.

Erikson, E. 1963, *Childhood and Society,* Norton, New York.

_____, 1968, *Identity Youth and Crisis,* Norton, New York.

Evans, D. 1996, *Dictionary of Lacanian Psychoanalysis,* Routledge, London.

Fanon, F. 2008, *Black Skin, White Masks,* Grove, New York.

Fairbairn, W.R.D. 1952, *Psychoanalytic Studies of the Personality,* London, Routledge.

Frankl, V., 1958, *Man's Search for Meaning,* Simon and Schuster, New York.

_____, 1965, *The Doctor and the Soul,* Simon and Schuster, New York.

_____, 1967, *Psychotherapy and Existentialism,* Simon and Schuster, New York.

_____, 1969, *The Will to Meaning,* Simon and Schuster, New York.

_____, 1975, *The Unconscious God,* Simon and Schuster, New York.

Frazier, J. 2006, *The Golden Bough*, NuVision.

Freud, S. 1900, *The Interpretation of Dreams,* Avon, New York, 1965

_____, (1946) *The Ego and the Id*. London, Hogarth Press.

_____, 2003, *The Uncanny,* Penguin, New York.

_____, 1975, *Group Psychology and the Analysis of the Ego*, Norton.

Fromm, E. 1955, *The Sane Society,* Rinehart, New York.

_____, 1941, *Escape from Freedom,* Holt, Rinehart and Winston, New York.

_____. 1961, *Marx's Concept of Man,* Ungar, New York.

Fukuyama, F., 2006, *The End of History and the Last Man,* Free Press

Gage, D., Morse, P., and Piechowski, M.., 1978, Measuring Levels of Emotional Development, *Genetic Psychology Monographs,* 1981; 103;129 –152.

Ganzerain, R. 1989, *Object Relations Group Psychotherapy, Group as an Object, a Tool and a Training Base.* IUP, New York.

Gilligan, C., 1982, *In a Different Voice,* Harvard University Press, Cambridge, MA.

Guntrip, H. 1969, *Schizoid Phenomena, Object Relations, and the Self,* IUP, New York.

Grant, U. S., 1999, *Personal Memoirs: U. S. Grant,* Modern Library.

Grotstein, J. and Rinsley, D., 1994, *Fairbairn and the Origins of Object Relations,* Guilford, New York and London.

Guerin, P., 1976, *Family Therapy, Theory and Practice,* Gardner Press.

Harris, A. T.s. Eliot's Mental Hygeine, *Journal of Modern Literature*.

Hartmann, E., 1991, *Boundaries in the Mind*, Basic Books, New York.

Hazell, C.G., 1984a, "Experienced levels of Emptiness and Existential Concern with different levels of Emotional Development and Profile of Values," *Psychological Reports*, 1984, 55, 967-976.

_____, 1984b, "Scale for Measuring Experienced Levels of Emptiness and Existential Concern," *Journal of Psychology*, 1984, 117, 177-182.

_____, 1989, "Levels of Emotional Development with Experienced Levels of Emptiness and Existential Concern," *Psychological Reports*, 1989, 64, 835-838.

_____, *Alterity and the theory of positive Disintegration: an organizing template*. Proceedings of Dabrowski Conference, University of Calgary, Alberta, August 2006.

_____, 2003, *The Experience of Emptiness*, Authorhouse, Bloomington IN.

_____, 2005a, *Imaginary Groups*, Authorhouse, Bloomington IN.

_____, 2005b, *Family Systems Activity Book*, Authorhouse, Bloomington, IN.

Hegel, G. F. W. (1807) 1977, *Phenomenology of Spirit*, Oxford U. P., London

Heidegger, M., 1927, *Sein und Zeit*, Erste Halfte, Max Niemeyer Verlag, Halle.

Heider, K. 2006, *Seeing Anthropology: Cultural Anthropology Through Film*, Allyn and Bacon.

Hoeller, S., 1989, *The Gnostic Jung and the Seven Sermons to the Dead*, Quest Books.

Hoffer, W., 1951, *Oral Aggressiveness and Ego Development*, Int. Jo. Psycho. Anal., 31; 156-160.

Hopkins, G. M. (1953) *Poems and Prose*, Penguin, London

Hopper, E. 2003, *Traumatic Experience in the Unconscious Life of Groups*. Jessica Kingsley Publishers.

Horkheimer, M. and Adorno, T., 2002, *The Dialectic of Enlightenment*, Stanford University Press.

Iacoboni, M. 2008, *Mirroring People*, Farrar, Strauss and Giroux, New York.

Jacobson, E. 1964, *The Self and the Object World*, International Universities Press, New York.

James, W. 1978, *The Writings of William James: A Comprehensive Edition*, Phoenix Press.

Janis, I. 1989, *Crucial Decisions*, Free Press.

Jung, C.G. (1971) *The Archetypes and the Collective Unconscious*. Princeton University Press.

_____, 1993, *Basic Writings of C. G. Jung*, Modern Library.

Kafka, F., 1926, *Das Schloss*, Kurt Wolff Verlag, Munchen.

_____, 1925, *Der Prozess,* Verlag Die Schmeide, Berlin.

_____, 1927, *Amerika,* Kurt Wolff Verlag, Munchen.

_____, 2006, *The Metamophsis,*Walking Lion Press.

Kant, I. 2001, *Basic Writings of Immanuel Kant,* Modern Library Classics.

Kernberg, O., 1975, *Borderline Conditions and Pathological Narcissism,* New York, Jason Aronson.

_____, 1976, *Object Relations Theory and Clinical Psychoanalysis,* New York,

Jason Aronson.

Kerttula, A. 2000, *Antler on the Sea: The Yupik and Chukchi of the Russian Far East,* Cornell University Press.

Kierkegaard, S., 1843, *Fear and Trembling,* Princeton University Press, 1954.

_____, 1846, *Two Ages,* Princeton University Press, 1978.

_____, 1849, *The Sickness Unto Death,* Princeton University Press, 1968.

Klein, M. 1935/1964, "A Contribution to the Psychogenesis of Manic-Depressive States," *Contributions to Psychoanalysis.* McGraw Hill, New York.

_____, 1946, "Notes on Some Schizoid Mechanisms," in *Writings of Melanie Klein, Volume 3, Envy and Gratitude and Other Works,* Hogarth Press, London.

_____, (2002) *Envy and Gratitude.* New York, Free Press.

Kohut, H. 1971, *The Analysis of the Self,* I.U.P., New York.

_____, 1977, *The Restoration of the Self,* I.U.P., New York.

Kojeve, A., 1969 (1947), *Introduction to the Reading of Hegel,* Cornell U. P. Ithaca and London.

Kowinski, J. S., 1985, *The Malling of America,* Xlibris Corporation.

Kuhn, T., 1996, *The Structure of Scientific Revolutions,* University of Chicago Press.

Lacan, J. 1977, *Ecrits, A Selection,* Norton, New York.

_____, 1981, *The Four Fundamental Concepts of Psychoanalysis,* Norton, New York.

_____, 1993, *The Seminar of Jacques Lacan: Book Three: The Psychoses,* Norton, New York.

Laplanche, J. 1999, *Essays on Otherness.* London, Routledge.

Laing, R. 1969, *The Divided Self,* Pantheon, New York.

Langs, R. 1978, *The Listening Process,* Jason Aronson, New York.

Laszlo, E., 1969, *System, Structure, and Experience,* Gordon and Breach, New York

Lao-tsu, *Tao Teh Ching,* (trans. Aleister Crowley), 1976, Askin Pubs., London.

Lawrence, W. Gordon., 2007, *Infinite Possibilities of Social Dreaming,* Karnac, London.

LeBon, G., 2002, *The Crowd,* Dover Publications.

Lefort, R., 1994, *Birth of the Other,* University of Illinois Press, Urbana and Chicago.

Levinas, E. 2000, *Alterity and Transcendence.* New York, Columbia University Press.

_____. 1969, *Totality and Infinity,* Duquesne, Pittsburgh, PA.

_____, 1987, *Time and the Other,* Duquesne, Pittsburgh, PA.

_____, 2006, *Humanism of the Other,* University of Illinois, Urbana and Chicago.

Levinson, D., 1978, *The Seasons of a Man's Life,* Knopf, New York.

Loevinger, J., 1976, *Ego Development,* Jossey Bass, San Francisco, CA.

Lopez-Corvo, R., 1995, *Self Envy,* Aronson, New York

Lowen, A., 1972, *Depression and the Body,* Penguin, New York.

Lyotard, J-F., 1984, *The Postmodern Condition,* University of Minnesota Press.

Mahler, M. 1975, *The Psychological Birth of the Human Infant,* Basic Books, New York.

Marcuse, H. 1964, *One Dimensional Man,* Beacon, Boston.

Marx, K., 1983, *The Portable Karl Marx,* (ed. Kamenka, E.) Viking Penguin, London.

Maslow, A., 1968, *Toward a Psychology of Being,* Van Nostrand, Princeton.

Masterson, J., 1972, *The Treatment of the Borderline Adolescent,* Wiley, New York.

May, R., 1950, *The Meaning of Anxiety,* Simon and Schuster, New York.

_____, 1953, *Man's Search for Himself,* Signet, Norton, New York.

McLuhan, M. 2003, *Understanding Media,* Gingko Press.

_____, 2005, *The Medium is the Massage,* Gingko Press.

_____, 1962, *The Gutenberg Galaxy: The Making of Typographic Man,* University of Toronto Press.

Menzies-Lyth, I., 1960, *A Case Study in the Functioning of Social Systems as a Defense Against Anxiety,* Human Relations, 13: 95-121.

Merleau-Ponty, M. 2003, *Maurice Merleau-Ponty: Basic Writings,* Ed. Thomas Baldwin, Routledge, New York.

Miller, A., 1981, *Prisoners of Childhood,* Basic Books, New York.

Minuchin, S., 1978, *Psychosomatic Families,* Harvard U.P. Cambridge, MA.

Mitchell, S. 1988, *Relational Concepts in Psychoanalysis,* Harvard University Press.

Miller, H., 1994, *Tropic of Cancer,* Grove Press.

_____, 1994, *Tropic of Capricorn, Grove Press.*

Miller, N. 2008, Emotion Management and Emotional Development: A Sociological Perspective. *In Dabrowski's Theory of Positive Disintegration,* Mendaglio, S. (ed). Great Potential Press, Scottsdale, AZ.

Musil, R., 1930, *The Man Without Qualities,* 1965, Capricorn, New York.

Nabokov, V. 1989, *Invitation to a Beheading,* Vintage.

Nietzsche, F., 1977, *The Portable Nietzsche,* Viking Press, New York.

Ogden, T. 1983, "The Concept of Internal Object Relations," in *Fairbairn and the Origins of Object Relations,* eds. Grotstein, J. and Rinsley, D., Guilford, New York (1994)

Ogburn, M. K., 1976, *Differentiating Guilt According to Theory of Positive Disintegration,* Unpublished doctoral Dissertation, University of Wisconsin-Madison, Counseling and Guidance.

Orwell, G., 2004, *Animal Farm,* 1st World Library.

Ouspensky, P. D. 1998, *Tertium Organum,* Kessinger.

Penguin Dictionary of Psychology (2002) Reber, a and E., Penguin, New York.

Pennington, 2002, *Social Psychology of Behavior in Small Groups,* Psychology Press, !st Edition.

Perls, F., 1965, *Gestalt Therapy Verbatim,* Real People Press, Lafayette, CA.

_____, 1973, *The Gestalt Approach and Eyewitness to Therapy,* Bantam, New York.

Pessoa, F. 2001, *The Book of Disquiet,* Penguin, London.

Piaget, J. 1976, *Piaget Sampler,* ed. Sarah Campbell, Wiley, New York.

Piaget, J. and Inhelder, B. 1969, *The Psychology of the child,* Basic Books, New York.

Piechowski, M., Silverman, L., Cunningham, K., Falk, R., *A Comparison of Intellectually Gifted and Artists on Five Dimensions of Mental Functioning,* Paper Presented at the American Educational Research Association Annual Meeting, March 1982, New York.

Pinel, J. 2006, *Biopsychology,* Pearson, Boston.

Poe, E.A. , 2003, *The Complete Works of Edgar Allan Poe,* Castle Books.

Popper, K., 2002, *The Logic of Scientific Discovery,* Routledge, London.

Rank, O., 1941, *Beyond Psychology,* Dover, New York.

Reich, W. 1933, *Character Analysis,* Orgone Institute Press, New York.

_____, 1942, *The Function of the Orgasm,* Orgoe Institute Press, NewYork.

Rice, A.K., 1965, *Learning for Leadership,* Tavistock, London

Ricoeur, P., 1970, *Freud and Philosophy: An Essay on Interpretation,* Yale, New Haven, CT.

_____,1995, *Oneself as Another.* Chicago, University of Chicago Press.

Rimbaud, A. 2008, *Arthur Rimbaud: Complete Works,* Harper Perennial.

Robert, J., Piechowski, M., 1980, "Two Types of Emotional and Intellectual Overexcitability: Conserving and Transforming," *Theory of Positive Disintegration Proceedings of the Third International Conference,* ed. Norbert John Duda, 1981, University of Miami, FL.

Rodier, P.M., 2000, The Early Origins of Autism, *Scientific American*, Feb., 284, 56-63.

Rogers, C. 1961, *On Becoming a Person,* Houghton Mifflin, Boston, MA.

Romanyshin, Robert, 1989, *Technology as Symptom and Dream,* Routledge, New York.

Rorty, R., 2000, *Philosophy and Social Hope,* Penguin, London.

_____,1981, *Philosophy and the Mirror of Nature,* Princeton University Press.

Rosenfeld, H., 1965, *Psychotic States,* Hogarth, London

Ross-Fryer, D., 2004, *The Intervention of the Other,* Other Press Professional.

Ruiz, Don-Miguel, 2008, *The Four Agreements,* Amber-Allen.

Salinger, J. D. 2001, *The Catcher in the Rye,* Back Bay Books.

Sartre, J.P., 1956, *Being and Nothingness,* Philosophical Library, New York.

_____, 1938, *La Nausee,* Gallimard, Paris.

_____, 1987, *Huis Clos,* Routledge, New York.

Saussure, F. la, 1998, *A Course in General Linguistics,* Open Court.

Schactel, E., 1959, *Metamorphosis,* Basic Books, New York.

Schact, R., 1970, *Alienation,* Anchor, New York.

Searles, H., 1979, *Countertransference,* IUP, New York.

_____, 1960, *The Nonhuman Environment in Normal Development and Schizophrenia,* IUP, New York.

Semmelhack, D., Hazell, C. and Hoffmann, W., (2008) The impact of group as a whole work on anxiety and depression in a severely mentally ill population. *The Journal for Specialists in Group Work.* 33. 43-60.

Shah, I., 1991, *The Way of the Sufi,* Penguin Arkana, London.

Skinner, B. F. 1976, *About Behaviorism,* Vintage.

Spitz, R., 1965, *The First Year of Life,* IUP, New York

Stanley, T. 1701, *History of Philosophy,* (2006) Apocryphile Press, Berkeley, CA.

Stevenson, R. L. 2002, *The Strange Case of Dr. Jekyll and Mr. Hyde,* Norton Critical Editions.

Sullivan, H. S., 1953, *Interpersonal Theory of Psychiatry,* Norton, New York.

Suzuki, D., 1956, *Zen Buddhism,* Anchor, New York.

Taussig, M. 1992, *Mimesis and Alterity.* London, Routledge.

Tillich, P., 1952, *The Courage to Be,* Yale University Press.

Tustin, F., 1972, *Autism and Childhood Psychoses,* Hogarth, London

_____, 1990, *The Protective Shell in Children and Adults,* Karnac, London.

Upanishads, The (Sri Isopanisad), (1997), The Bhaktivedanta Book Trust, Los Angeles, CA.

Vlastos, G., 1975, *Plato's Universe,* University of Washington Press, Seattle, WA.

Watson, J., 2008, *Behaviorism,* West Press.

Winnicott, D. W., 1960, "Ego Distortion in Terms of True and False Self," in *The Maturational Processes and the Facilitating Environment,* pp 140-152, Hogarth, London.

_____, 1964, *The Child, The Family, and the Outside World,* Pelican, New York.

_____, 1965a, *The Maturational Processes and the Facilitating Environment,* IUP, New York.

_____, 1965b, *The Family and Individual Development,* Tavistock Publications, London.

_____, 1971a, *Therapeutic Consultations in Child Psychiatry,* Hogarth, London

_____, 1971b, *Playing and Reality,* Basic Books, New York.

Wittgenstein, L., 2001, *Tractatus Logico-Philosophicus,* Routledge Classics, New York.

Yeats, W. B., 1989, "The Second Coming" in *Collected Poems of W. B. Yeats,* Finneran, R.J. (ed), Macmillan, New York

Zizek, S., 1993, *Looking Awry,* MIT, Cambridge, MA

Zimmer, K. 2005, The Neurobiology of the Self, *Scientific American,* Nov, Ps 92 - 101

Music Cited

Byrds, The, 2006, *Eight Miles High,* Magic.

Lennon, John, 2002, *The Songs of John Lennon; The Beatle Years,* Berklee Press.

The Police, 1983, *Sychronicity,* A and M

Movies Cited

The Discreet Charm of the Bourgeoisie, 2002, (1972), Director Luis Bunuel, Criterion.

The Double Life of Veronique, 2006, Director, Krzysztof Kieslowski.

Fat Girl, 2004, Director, Catherine Breillat.

!Nai, the Story of !Kung Woman, 1980, John Marshall and Adrienne Meismer, Documentary Educational Resources.

The Others, 2001. Director, Alejandro Amenabar.

A Talking Picture, 2004, Director, Manoel de Oliveira.

Trobriand Cricket, An Ingenious Response to Colonialism, 1976, Gary Kildea and Gerry Leach, Berkeley Media.